Florida History

by Hal Bamford

GREAT OUTDOORS

PUBLISHING CO.

4747 TWENTY-EIGHTH STREET NORTH
ST. PETERSBURG, FLORIDA 33714

2nd Edition

ISBN: 0-8200-1032-4

Photo Acknowledgments: Grateful acknowledgment is given to the Robert Manning Strozier Library, Tallahassee, Florida, for many of the photographs used in this book.

Printed in United States of America

Contents

Part		page
I	Florida's Indians and First White Settlers The Explorers— The First Settlements— Summary: Spain's Tenuous Hold— Work Section	1
II	International Rivalry in Florida The Picture Changes— Summary: Spain Loses Florida— Work Section	11
III	The Changing Fate of Florida The Changes— Florida in the Revolu- tion— Summary: English Ownership and Loss—Work Section	21
IV	Florida Under Spanish Rule Troubles Begin Early— In the West— Back in the East—Summary: Spain Loses Florida (Again)— Work Section	29
V	Florida Gains Statehood The Indian Situation—Florida Enters the Union— Summary: Florida, the State — Work Section	39
VI	Florida Leaves the Union and Returns Secession and War Begin— As the War Ended— Summary: How the War Changed Florida— Work Section	47
VII	A Period of Growth: Tourism Begins Growth of the Railroads—Railroad Tycoons— Florida and the Spanish-American War— Summary: Development Begins— Work Section	57
VIII	Twentieth Century Florida The Growth of Aviation— The Roaring Twenties— Florida In World War II— The Space Age—Summary: Florida Today — Work Section	65
	Index	75

From the Author

Florida is one of the most unusual of the 50 United States.

Within the boundaries of the state are the oldest continuously occupied city on the North American continent, the only state capital of the Confederate States of America which went uncaptured by Union troops during the Civil War and the launching site of the first manned trip to the moon.

The men and women who have contributed to the more than 400 years of history often have been controversial and always colorful.

Today, Florida is the fastest growing state in the United States and many of the residents are people who were born in other parts of the nation or in foreign countries.

For that reason, a large percentage of the state's new residents do not understand the rich history which makes the state so unusual nor are they familiar with many who have contributed to that history.

Therefore, the author feels this book has a special place for our younger citizens, not only in helping them to understand the past but also in helping the younger generation to continue the policies that have helped to make Florida the fine place it is in which to live.

I hope you enjoy your exploration into Florida's past and your look at the people who have contributed to the state's history.

HAL BAMFORD

Part I

Florida's Indians and First White Settlers

INDIANS IN FLORIDA

Most historians do not agree as to when the first Indians arrived in what is now called Florida nor do they agree on the way in which they arrived.

Some insist the first redmen came to the peninsula as long as 20,000 years ago, arriving over a land bridge which then connected Asia and the North American continent.

Others are equally certain Indians did not live in Florida before 10,000 years ago and feel that the Indians probably arrived from Central and South America by way of canoes.

Whenever and however the arrival may have occurred, it is almost certain those early Indians were hunters. They used the flesh of animals for their food, their skins for clothing and bones for tools and ornaments.

Many bands of Indians lived along the coast and they quickly discovered the sea was also a plentiful source of food. There are many sites throughout the state which show evidence of shell mounds, made when the redmen discarded oysters and the shells of other shellfish, building huge mounds. It is believed these mounds may have had religious significance to the Indians.

MEANING OF FLORIDA INDIAN PLACE NAMES

Alachua...sink hole
Alafia...hunting river
Apalachicola...place of the ruling people
Apopka...potato eating place
Apoxsee...tomorrow
Bithlo...canoe
Caloosahatchee... **river** of the Calusas
Chassahowitzka...pumpkin opening place
Chattahoochee...marked stones
Chuluota...pine island
Econfina...natural bridge
Fenholloway...high bridge
Hialeah...prairie
Hickpochee...little prairie
Homosassa...place of peppers
Hypoluxo...round mound
Iamonia...peaceful
Immokalee...tumbling water
Istokpoga...dead man
Istachatta...red man

Lochloosa...black dipper
Lokossee...bear
Loxahatchee...turtle creek
Miami...big water
Micanopy...head chief
Miomi...bitter water
Ocala...spring
Ochlockonee...yellow water
Okahumpka...one water or pond
Okaloosa...black water
Oklawaha...muddy or boggy
Osceola...black Indian drink
Okeechobee...big water
Ochopee...big field
Opalockee...big swamp
Pahokee...grassy water
Palatka...ferry crossing
Panasoffkee...deep valley
Pennawa...turkey
Seminole...wild man, runaway

Sopchoppy...long twisted stream
Steinhatchee...dead man's creek
Tallahassee...old town
Telogia...palmetto
Thonotosassa...place of flints
Thopekaliga...fort site
Tsala Apopka...trout eating place
Umatilla...water rippling over sand
Wacahoota...cow house or barn
Wausau...hunting place
Weekiwachee...little spring
Welaka...river of lakes
Wewahitchka...water view
Wetappo...broad stream
Wimco...chief water
Withlacoochee...little big water
Yalaha...orange
Yeehaw...wolf

Indian place names; the names are capsule descriptions of the areas.

THE MAIN TRIBES

It is almost impossible to determine how many different tribes once roamed throughout Florida but, by the time the white man began arriving from Europe, there were no more than three main tribes remaining.

In the southern part of the state, from an area just south of the city of Sarasota on the Gulf coast and Cape Canaveral on the Atlantic coast, the Calusa tribe lived. Some historians say they were the most fierce and hostile race of Indians in North America. Other tribes which existed in this area probably were subject to this powerful group.

Between the northern boundary of the Calusa's land and the Suwannee River in the northern part of the state, the Timucua or Utina Indians held a similar position of power over lesser tribes.

The other main group of Indians in Florida was the Apalachee tribe. It was the most powerful in the area which we call the Panhandle.

When white men began arriving, they came into contact with all of these tribes. Some tribes were wiped out because of war, mistreatment as slaves or death from white man's diseases.

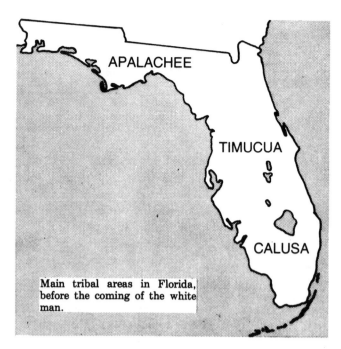

Main tribal areas in Florida, before the coming of the white man.

Others were brought under control of the white men through religious conversion. These attempts to convert the Indians to Christianity had a great influence on the white man's moving into the interior of the state as will be explained later in this section.

The Explorers

Just as historians do not agree on when the first Indians arrived, they do not agree on when the first European explorer arrived in the western hemisphere nor do they agree on who it might have been.

However, it is known that when people like the Cabots, Christopher Columbus and Amerigo Vespucci returned to Europe after seeing this area, they told stories which were wondrous to their listeners. Those stories made more people want to come to the western hemisphere.

To most Europeans, life in the early years of the 16th century was drab and colorless in their homelands. Sailing with an explorer could open new and exciting possibilities for them. To other adventurers, landing in the new world meant the possibility of attaining riches such as they had only dreamed of before.

True tales of such adventures were exciting. Adding a few white lies made them even more so. Soon, adventurers by the hundreds were seeking to join those

who could afford to sponsor an expedition. Even the lowliest of peasants could dream of the day the new world would bring fame and wealth.

JUAN PONCE DE LEON

A Spanish nobleman-soldier, Juan Ponce de Leon, came to the new world on Columbus' second voyage in 1493. On arrival in Hispaniola, he led a military conquest of that island and became its governor. When Columbus returned to Spain, Ponce stayed behind.

Tales of other islands were brought to him. One was of Puerto Rico, an island said to be much richer than his. He gathered a new force, sailed there and conquered it in 1509 and, once again, became its governor.

During these years, Ponce became a rich man. But, his thirst for adventure still burned bright and got stronger as still more tales of other wonders were brought to him. One of those tales was of a land called Bimini, richer than any other in the area and possessed

2

Ponce de Leon had one great dream in life—to find the Fountain of Youth. But whether he desired eternal youth, fame, or the money such a discovery would make for him is not clear. What do you think?

of wonderful waters, called the Fountain of Youth. One drink from this magical fountain would make the person young forever, and he would never die.

He became determined to find this land. In 1512, Diego Columbus, son of the explorer with whom Ponce had come to the new world, arrived in Puerto Rico to become its governor. Ponce was now free to seek Bimini. He outfitted three ships with the wealth he had accumulated and, on March 3, 1513, sailed to new adventures.

NAMING OF FLORIDA

After sailing to many islands and not finding the fabled fountain, Ponce turned westward. In a few days, he sighted land. What he saw was the shore of Florida.

No one is certain exactly where he finally landed, although most agree it was probably between the present-day city of St. Augustine and the mouth of the St. Johns River.

All historians do agree he named the land "Pascua Florida." In Spanish, it meant "Feast of the Flowers." The land, bursting with lush greenery and flowers of every color, was sighted on Easter Sunday. A pious man, Ponce named the county for its flowers and the religious holiday.

The white man had arrived in Florida.

CONTACT WITH INDIANS

Ponce did not find his Fountain of Youth. He did find Indians and he soon learned they were hostile to the white man.

This was one of the things he made plain to the king of Spain when he returned to Europe. He also felt they could become friendly if they were taught about the white man's God and suggested priests accompany expeditions which would set up colonies in Florida. This suggestion would have a great influence on the Spanish period in Florida's history.

Ponce wanted to return to Florida and found a settlement. However, the king was more interested in using his experience in the islands and sent him off to conquer others in the Caribbean.

It was 1521 before Ponce was ready to return to Florida. That year, with two ships and 200 colonists, he landed on the Gulf coast and began selecting a site for his settlement.

His dream was never achieved.

Indians, probably the fierce Calusa, attacked his landing party, killed several of his followers and wounded Ponce. The survivors were forced to return to their ships and sail for Puerto Rico. There, shortly after they arrived, Ponce died of the wounds the Indians had inflicted.

PANFILO DE NARVAEZ

Ponce's death did not discourage others. Several Spanish adventurers touched land in North America in the next few years but most sought only gold and other wealth.

It was not until 1527 the next effort to establish a colony was made.

The man who made that attempt was almost as familiar with the new world as Ponce had been.

In 1520, a year before Ponce returned to Florida, the king of Spain had sent Panfilo de Narvaez to New Spain in Mexico to arrest another adventurer — Hernando Cortez — who had fallen into disfavor. However, when Narvaez arrived, Hernando Cortez refused to submit. A fight ensued; Narvaez was wounded and lost an eye. He would spend the next six years with Cortez and, in that time, become a friend. More important, he would learn many things about the new world.

In spite of the fact he did not accomplish the king's mission, when he returned to Spain in 1526, he was rewarded with the right to return to the new world and establish a colony in Florida.

NARVAEZ IN FLORIDA

When he left Spain, his ships carried about 600 colonists and soldiers. On the trip, however, storms caused two of his ships to be lost and, by the time he reached Florida in 1528, his company had been reduced to about 400 men.

Unlike Ponce, Narvaez' followers had little trouble with the Indians.

The first day Narvaez landed, near what is now St. Petersburg, he found a deserted Indian village. The next morning, the Indians returned. They told wonderful stories of much gold to the north but denied they had any. Narvaez believed them. He planned to march to that village and find that wealth.

THE MARCH NORTH

To be sure his ships would be available to load all that gold he was sure he would find, he divided his force. Part of them sailed north along the coast with the ships. The rest marched north with their leader. After a long and difficult trip overland, the marchers finally reached an Indian village called Apalachee. Once again, however, there was no gold.

Disappointed, Narvaez sent part of his band to the coast to find the ships he believed awaited them. Despite many visits and weeks of waiting, the ships never arrived. No one today knows what happened to them. They were never seen again.

Narvaez decided he and his followers would have to build boats of their own. He knew Mexico, where he had spent six years, was west of them. They would try to reach that Spanish country.

The trip took them along the Gulf coast, all the way to Texas. There, a storm overtook the tiny boats and most of the men died. A few managed to reach the shore, in what is now the state of Texas, and continued their journey by land. Eight years after they had landed in Florida, three survivors reached New Spain in Mexico.

Narvaez was not one of them. He died during the wandering. Cabeza de Vaca was. He would return to Spain and, with his stories, influence many others.

HERNANDO DE SOTO

Like his most famous predecessors, Hernando de Soto was no stranger to the new world.

He had been a member of Francisco Pizarro's party during that leader's earlier conquest of Peru in South America. Back in Spain, he became acquainted with de Vaca and his travels and began planning an expedition of his own.

In 1538, two years after de Vaca had returned home, de Soto fitted out a new expedition. Again, the destination was Florida. Based on de Vaca's tales, he planned to follow much the same route as Narvaez.

His expedition first touched land somewhere in the area that is now called Tampa Bay and began a march that also would end in his death.

THE CHIEF'S DAUGHTER

Shortly after he came ashore, however, a strange experience confronted him. He sent a group of his men out to scout the area and they came into contact with a band of Indians. As they prepared to attack, one of the "Indians" cried out to them in Spanish.

Charles V, the King of Spain, appointed Hernando de Soto (above) to "conquer, pacify, and populate the northern continent." The Indians de Soto encountered met his demands for food, carriers, and guides with hostility.

The man identified himself as Juan Ortiz and he told an almost unbelievable tale.

He explained that he had been a member of the Narvaez expedition but had been captured by the Indians and became a slave. Weakened by months of heavy work for his captors, the chief felt he had lived out his usefulness and decided to put him to death.

However, the chief's daughter had fallen in love with him, he explained, and at the last minute she came to his rescue. He had lived as a member of the tribe ever since.

Ortiz had other tales to tell. He explained to de Soto that he had heard his Indian captors talk of rich cities and much gold to the north. The information strengthened de Soto's resolve and he turned his expedition northward and marched off.

Unlike Narvaez, who took to boats in northern Florida, de Soto continued beyond the Indian village of Apalachee. His wanderings took him into what we now know as Georgia, South Carolina, Tennessee and, eventually, to the Mississippi River. There, however, his stamina ran out, he died and his followers buried him beneath the waters of that river.

The First Settlements

Failure of the de Soto expedition closed more than 30 years of fruitless efforts by Spanish explorers in Florida. Hundreds of men had sailed to the new world. Most of them had died. No riches had been found. No permanent settlement had been established.

Spain's rulers began to lose interest. Expeditions from Spain stopped but all interest did not die.

New Spain was a thriving area in Mexico and the spirit of adventure remained strong where the fruits of successful settlement were evident every day.

In March 1559, a gentleman who had won fame exploring Spanish claims north of Mexico — in what is now southwestern United States — began assembling a group of more than 1,500 soldiers and civilians to found a colony of his own.

By June, his expedition was ready and he sailed from Veracruz on June 11, 1559. His destination was Ochuse Bay, a body of water we now call Pensacola Bay. His name was Tristan de Luna.

TRISTAN DE LUNA

Troubled by storms and lack of enough provisions, only part of the group completed the trip. They arrived on August 14, 1559, chose a site for their settlement and began building a town. De Luna kept about 80 people at the city site to work and sent the rest inland in search of food.

The Indians, anxious to keep their food for the winter ahead, resisted pleas to share. De Luna, determined to stay, dispatched part of his fleet to Mexico to get additional supplies. Those that remained on the island soon began to argue amongst themselves. Storms blew up to help destroy what had been created.

For more than a year and a half, the settlement struggled to survive. Then new ships arrived from Mexico with supplies and the news de Luna had been replaced by a new leader. He left but dissatisfaction had grown so strong that, within a few more weeks, the colony was abandoned.

FRENCH EFFORTS

Now, even the enthusiasm for Florida weakened in Mexico. The failure of de Luna's colony did nothing to improve the feeling in Spain. Then, actions of a rival nation changed the attitude once again.

Although Florida appeared useless, Spain continued to take great riches from its settlements in Mexico and South America. Her colonies there were too strong to be attacked but the French felt there must be a way they could capture at least a portion of the wealth as it was shipped to Spain.

An admiral of France, Gaspard de Coligny, convinced the French king he had the answer to the problem. He explained, he could plant a settlement in Florida and, from that base, stage raids on Spain's gold-laden ships before they started across the Atlantic.

The first effort was made late in April 1562 when three ships and 150 Frenchmen, under command of Jean Ribault, arrived at the mouth of the St. Johns River. They established a small colony there but were forced to abandon it when provisions ran out.

Two years later, the French tried again. This time they sent 300 men and four women and their commander was Rene Goulaine de Laudonniere. Ribault was also in the group. They established Fort Caroline, five miles up river from their previous settlement.

Rene Goulaine de Laudonniere headed France's second attempt to colonize Florida. His group of 300 settlers included soldiers, sailors, and servants, but no farmers. Would farmers be important to a settlement attempt?

THE SPANISH ANSWER

When word of this colony reached Spain's King Philip II, he commissioned Pedro Menendez de Aviles to sail to Florida. He was to start a permanent colony and destroy that of the French.

In August 1565, he arrived in Florida with 500 soldiers, 200 sailors and 100 civilians. He put many ashore with instructions to begin building a city. Then, with most of his soldiers, he sailed for the French settlement to carry out his other orders.

While he was gone, the Spaniards began their town. They named it St. Augustine, in honor of the festival of San Augustin, a Spanish religious celebration, observed the day of their arrival.

In the next few days, in a series of bloody fights, Menendez captured the French fort on the St. Johns, routed the soldiers and pursued and murdered most of them as they fled along the coastline.

After the French threat had been eliminated, all efforts were turned to building at St. Augustine. Although progress was slow and many problems constantly were encountered, the settlement slowly grew and became stronger.

Although the road was hard, today St. Augustine stands as the oldest city of continued occupation in North America.

THE MISSIONS

Despite its growth, it was evident to everyone that the Indians must be made friendly if the settlement was to survive. There had to be assurance they would not attack and that if other Europeans did, the Indians would help the Spanish in St. Augustine defend themselves.

The answer seemed to be to convert the redmen to Christianity.

Beginning early in the 1600s, more and more missionaries were sent to Florida and, in 1612, the Bishop of Cuba created a province of Santa Elena, which included all of what we now know as Florida, Georgia and South Carolina.

As the missionary population grew, priests began moving inland from the coast, establishing missions from which to teach and convert the Indians with whom they came in contact.

By the middle of the 1600s, they had established a chain of such missions which extended all the way from St. Augustine to the Apalachicola River, almost halfway across Florida's Panhandle.

Pedro Menendez de Aviles was commissioned to "explore and colonize Florida." As part of his efforts to drive out non-Spaniards, he destroyed France's weakly guarded Ft. Caroline.

6

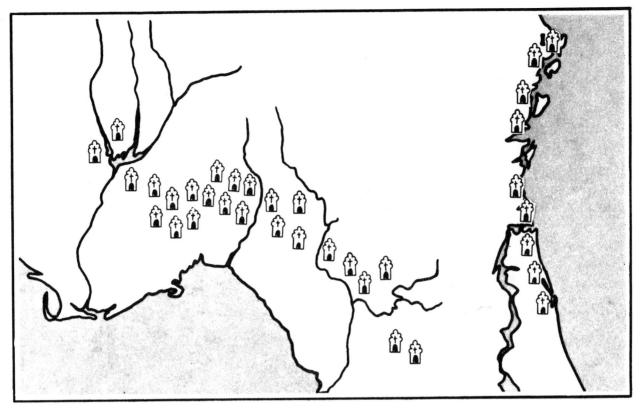

In order to convert Florida's Indians, Spain established a line of missions across northern Florida.

In the meantime, the French, who had been chased from Florida, had not given up all efforts in the new world. Moreover, they were having considerably greater success elsewhere.

For example, they established many settlements along the St. Lawrence River, between what is now Canada and the United States. From these, they moved west to the Mississippi River and down it all the way to the Gulf of Mexico.

Once they reached the Gulf, the French were again in a position to threaten Spanish Florida. Most exposed, of course, were the many missions, all unarmed, which stretched across the middle of the Spanish claim.

FOUNDING OF PENSACOLA

Once again, Spain was forced to act in defense of what was already established.

From Mexico, the Spanish sent out expeditions to search for the French. One of these accidentally rediscovered Ochuse Bay — the Bay of Pensacola — where, almost 150 years earlier, de Luna had founded his short-lived colony.

Realizing the French were moving in that direction, the Spanish decided to try once more to establish a settlement there.

In November 1698, a group, under command of Juan Jordan, arrived in the bay and began building a fort and city of thatched palm huts. The work went well and it was well for Spain that it did.

Shortly after they had become strong enough to defend themselves, a French expedition sailed into view. The French stopped, observed the Spanish defense works and decided they did not have the strength to challenge them.

They chose to continue on westward to establish other settlements.

SEEDS OF TROUBLE

Thus, by the end of the 17th century, the Spanish had permanent, fortified settlements in St. Augustine on the Atlantic coast and in Pensacola on the Gulf coast. In between there were a number of isolated and unarmed missions. As allies, most of the Indians in Florida were friendly to the Spanish.

Aside from this very thinly populated area, Spain had little to protect herself in Florida. What made the situation even more dangerous was Spain's neighbors in the new world.

To the north, the British colonies were growing much more rapidly than settlements in Spanish America. To the west, the French had moved as close as what we now know as Mobile, Alabama.

In Europe, wars between the mother nations were almost constant. It, therefore, was inevitable that the colonies in the new world would not be able to live in peace while wars raged in Europe.

Summary: Spain's Tenuous Hold

The first 200 years after discovery of the new world, Florida's history belonged almost completely to Spain. It was a period of exploration first, followed by attempted settlement. Nearly 50 years passed, however, between the time the first explorers arrived and the first permanent settlement finally was established.

Once the town of St. Augustine was born, the Spanish began to spread into other parts of Florida but that spread was slow and only missions were established. They served a purpose by making friends of the Indians but they were not strong enough to defend ownership of the land.

It was nearly 150 years after St. Augustine was established that a new threat by the French forced the Spanish to build another fortified town to defend their claims. That town was Pensacola.

As 200 years of history ended, Spain had accomplished very little in comparison with European settlements in other parts of North America. But, weak as Spain was in Florida, she was there alone in 1700.

That condition was soon destined to change.

Work Section

TRUE-FALSE

Answer the following questions true or false.

1. Historians know exactly when the first Indians arrived in what we now call Florida.
2. The Calusa Indians are believed to have been the most fierce and hostile tribe that ever lived in North America.
3. Juan Ponce de Leon named the land we now call Florida.
4. Panfilo de Narvaez landed where St. Petersburg now stands.
5. Ochuse Bay is the body of water we now call Boca Ciega Bay.
6. Pensacola was the first permanent Spanish settlement in Florida.
7. When Tristan de Luna settled Pensacola, the Indians helped him by supplying his followers with food.
8. The first French settlement in Florida was where the present city of St. Augustine stands.
9. Pedro Menendez de Aviles founded St. Augustine.
10. All of the Spanish missions were strong forts.

MULTIPLE CHOICE

Only one of the following answers is correct. Select the right one.

1. The first Indians arrived in Florida
   a. Over the Bering land bridge
   b. By boat
   c. No one knows for sure
   d. None of the above
2. By the time the white man arrived in Florida
   a. All of the Indians had disappeared
   b. Three main tribes ruled in different sections of the peninsula
   c. Only the Calusa Indians remained
   d. The Indians were very friendly
3. Juan Ponce de Leon
   a. Established the first settlement in Florida
   b. Found the Fountain of Youth
   c. Died of wounds received in a fight with the Indians
   d. Never saw Florida
4. Hernando de Soto
   a. Found Juan Ortiz
   b. Built Ft. De Soto
   c. Was the first Spanish explorer to march north in Florida
   d. Returned to Spain a hero
5. The French settlement on the St. Johns River
   a. Was the first in Florida
   b. Became the most successful in Florida
   c. Was built after St. Augustine
   d. Was named Fort Caroline
6. Spanish missionaries
   a. Were never allowed to come to Florida
   b. Established a number of missions among the Indians
   c. Made forts of all their missions
   d. None of the above

7. Juan Jordan
   a. Was the first Spaniard to see Pensacola Bay
   b. Sailed to Pensacola from Spain
   c. Was chased away from Pensacola Bay by the French
   d. None of the above
8. Panfilo de Narvaez
   a. Never returned to Spain
   b. Found great riches during his travels in Florida
   c. Landed near what we now call Key West
   d. Founded the first permanent settlement in Florida
9. By 1700, Spain had
   a. Established two permanent cities in Florida
   b. Controlled a number of missions
   c. Was friendly with the Indians
   d. All of the above
10. Pascua Florida means
    a. Feast of the Flowers
    b. Pensacola
    c. St. Augustine
    d. Spanish mission

COMPLETION

Fill in the blanks in the following sentences with the correct word or phrase.

1. The most powerful Indian tribe in the Panhandle area of Florida was the
2. _____ was the first Spaniard to land in Florida.
3. Panfilo de Narvaez lost _____ in a fight with Hernando Cortez.
4. Only _____ of Narvaez' followers eventually reached Mexico.
5. The first settlement in the Pensacola area was
6. _____ sponsored the first French attempt to place a colony in Florida.
7. St. Augustine was founded by
8. Spanish missionaries were sent to Florida to
9. The French wanted colonies in Florida so they could
10. By 1700, the only settlement in Florida belonged to

SUGGESTED WORK PROJECTS

A. Using a map of Florida, locate the following places and tell why they were important.
   1. St. Augustine
   2. Tallahassee
   3. The mouth of the St. Johns River
   4. Pensacola
   5. Santa Rosa Island
   6. The Apalachicola River
   7. Pensacola Bay
B. If possible, take your class on a field trip to one of the many shell mound areas which are found throughout Florida.
C. If possible, take your class on a field trip to the Fort Caroline monument near Jacksonville.
D. If possible take your class on a field trip to the old, restored section of St. Augustine.

Part II

International Rivalry in Florida

ENGLISH COLONIES

More than 40 years after St. Augustine became a permanent settlement, another colony was planted elsewhere in what later was to become the United States.

In 1607, Jamestown was founded in Virginia. Thirteen years later, in 1620, the Pilgrims landed at Plymouth in Massachusetts. Both were English colonies.

Unlike the Spanish efforts in Florida, however, the English colonies began expanding and others followed. Such success worried the Spanish because their own growth was not nearly so rapid.

Unfortunately, the Spanish position in Florida remained so weak they were able to do little more than worry about the growing British efforts. Then, in 1670, a new English colony was founded at Charles Town (now Charleston), South Carolina.

THE SEARLES RAID

What really frightened Spanish officials was the fact this colony gave the British a base from which to launch further raids such as one which had been sent against them in 1668.

This is how Spanish soldiers dressed in the 1660's. Is this sort of clothing practical for use in Florida? Why or why not?

11

In this earlier raid, Robert Searles, an Englishman whom the Spanish had long accused of piracy in Florida waters, captured two Spanish ships. In May, he used these ships to transport a raiding party to St. Augustine. He arrived in late afternoon and anchored just offshore. Spanish lookouts recognized the ships as their own and decided they were bringing supplies which would be brought into the harbor in the morning.

Instead, after darkness had fallen, Searles and his raiders came ashore and attacked the city. They killed more than 60 people, about one of every four Spaniards in the city, and burned many of the buildings.

Then, they returned to the ships and sailed off before the Spanish could get organized and return the attack.

CASTILLO DE SAN MARCOS

With this raid still fresh in their minds, the founding of Charles Town forced the Spanish finally to build a permanent fort to protect themselves. In 1672, two years after the founding of Charles Town, the Spanish began construction of the Castillo de San Marcos.

It was a huge, stone fortress, designed to protect the city from attack by land or by sea. Built of co-quina stone, it had walls 12 feet thick and was large enough to house 1,500 people.

The new fort greatly improved the defense of St. Augustine but it did little to protect Spanish settlements elsewhere in Florida.

TROUBLE AT THE MISSIONS

As explained in Part I, the Spanish had built a string of missions which reached halfway across Florida. Several of these were established along the Atlantic coast, reaching into areas we now know as Georgia and South Carolina.

The new British settlements, some just 50 miles to the north of these coastal missions, did not like the idea of the Spanish being that close.

The main reason for the missions was to convert the Indians to Christianity, win their friendship and use them to help defend Spanish claims.

The British settlers, richer and becoming stronger all the time, also wanted the Indians as friends. They were able to pay more in gifts and soon had the Indians working for them and against the Spanish.

By 1685, they had won such influence over the Indians, the redmen began raiding Spanish missions. They destroyed several, killed many of the missionaries and forced the Spanish to retreat southward along the coast, all the way to the St. Marys River before the raids ended.

One of the earliest photos of Ft. San Marcos (left) and a photo of the fort today (right). The older photo was taken during the Civil War while the fort was occupied by Union troops. Notice how the fort has been restored since that time.

Castillo de San Marcos is surrounded by a moat forty feet wide. The only entrance is across a drawbridge. The walls are thirteen feet thick at the base, and are made of coquina, a stone unique to Florida's east coast. How could such a fort be built without heavy machinery?

JAMES MOORE RAIDS

As British influence over the Indians continued to grow, Carolina Gov. James Moore decided the time had come to attack other Spanish missions in the interior of Florida.

However, before he attacked them, he felt he had to attack St. Augustine. If he could conquer the city, Spanish defense would be eliminated.

In November 1702, he sent a small group of men up the St. Johns River to a point near St. Augustine.

Moore brought the rest of his force south to the city by boat and the two groups met just north of St. Augustine.

The wisdom of building the fort now became quite clear. Although the British kept the people trapped in the fort continuously for almost two months and although they destroyed much of the town, they could not win a surrender. During this attack, the people in the

fort ate stored food and water.

Moore was forced to retreat to the Carolinas.

Although he had failed to knock out the main Spanish base, he realized he could hurt the Spanish efforts by attacking elsewhere. He decided to turn his attention to the chain of missions.

THE MISSION RAIDS

With only about 50 English volunteers but with more than 1,500 Indians to help, he marched toward Apalachee.

He began first at the point farthest from St. Augustine and attacked mission after mission. The Spanish, with almost no soldiers in the area, were unable to fight back successfully and almost all of the missions were destroyed or badly damaged.

However, despite this major loss, the Spanish did not abandon the area.

13

SAN MARCOS DE APALACHE

Many settlers remained and a few of the missionaries also stayed.

Most of the Spanish troubles which followed the Moore raids were with the Indians so it was decided to rebuild a fort which had been started many years before — San Marcos de Apalache.

San Marcos de Apalache was located where the St. Marks and Wakulla Rivers came together, about six miles from the Gulf of Mexico.

It had served as an early Spanish trading post from 1633 until 1682. On March 2, 1682, a group of pirates attacked the site and easily took it from the few Spanish soldiers stationed there. The pirates took everything that was movable and burned what they had to leave behind, after killing the Spanish soldiers. Because it was so far from everything, the Spanish had decided not to rebuild.

With the founding of Pensacola, opinions changed. Fort San Marcos would not be as isolated as in the past and would provide added help to priests and scattered settlers around the area now known as Tallahassee. In 1718, it was rebuilt and a larger group of soldiers was sent there.

In the next few years, it became a fairly important trading post. Indians came from north of the fort and pirate and Spanish trading ships stopped because of its good harbor. They all traded goods.

GROWING PENSACOLA

When Pensacola was founded in 1698, one of the most important men in the new colony was Jaime Franck. He was called the best military engineer in New Spain and quickly drew the plans and set about building Ft. San Carlos de Austria at the site of the new city.

His fort become particularly important when the French decided to found a city of their own on the Mobile River, named Mobile, less than 100 miles west of Pensacola, three years after Pensacola was founded.

At first, the city was located about 27 miles up the Mobile River but after the city was damaged by a flood in 1711 it was moved to its present site.

Fortunately for both the French and Spanish, the two towns remained friendly during their early days. Officials even traded food and supplies with each other, realizing both faced hostile Indians.

The Spanish had learned just how hostile the Indians could be in 1707. In that year, redmen, friendly to the British, attacked Pensacola and destroyed most of the city. The settlers remained safe in Jaime Franck's fort.

San Marcos de Apalache was a crumbling fort when this photo was taken during the Civil War. The building behind the soldiers was just 150 years old. What factors in Florida's climate would contribute to the destruction of a building such as this?

The Picture Changes

In 1719, the peaceful picture quickly changed.

The year before, peace in Europe once again had been shattered when Spain's King Philip began a move he hoped would also bring him to the throne of France.

At the same time, trying to please his Italian wife, Elizabeth Farnese, he sought to oust the Austrians from Italy and sent an army into Sardinia and Sicily.

These two actions led four European nations to join forces to stop him. England, France, Holland and Austria formed an alliance and, in August 1718, the War of the Quadruple Alliance was launched against Spain.

French forces in Europe invaded northern Spain and a British fleet came to the aid of Sicily.

FIGHTING IN FLORIDA

Word of the war reached the French settlement at New Orleans on April 13, 1719. Jean Baptiste Le Moyne, one of that settlement's leaders, quickly decided this was an excuse to seize Pensacola. He put together a small army, rushed it to Florida and surprised Spanish officials who were unaware of the war.

On May 14, 1719, the Spanish surrendered. Part of the terms included the fact the French would take the Spanish to Havana, Cuba. Word of the war had reached Cuba, however, and when the French ships arrived there, they were seized by the governor of Cuba.

Using these same ships, the Spaniards sent an army back to Pensacola. The French at that city, not realizing the ships had been captured, allowed them into the bay and, two days later, Pensacola had been recaptured.

Another month passed before a French fleet arrived at the settlement of Mobile. When they learned what had happened, they again attacked Pensacola and captured it once more, on September 18.

This time, the Spaniards were taken to Cuba and exchanged for the French prisoners captured on the earlier voyage.

Pensacola remained in French hands until a peace treaty was signed in Europe in 1721. By terms of that treaty, Pensacola was returned to Spain but stayed in possession of the Frenchmen until 1723.

Fortunately for the Spanish, the English in their settlements on the Atlantic seaboard were too occupied with their own growth to bother about St. Augustine during the war.

That situation also was about to change.

NEW ENGLISH ATTACKS

The English, slowly but steadily, moved south from the Carolinas, establishing a string of wooden forts, which by 1725, reached as far south as the Altamaha River, near the present-day city of Darien, S.C., less than 70 miles north of the St. Marys River.

These forts bothered the Spanish but their settlements still were so weak they could do little about attacking and driving the British back.

The forts also bothered the Indians and, shortly after Ft. King George, the site on the Altamaha, was completed, Indians attacked and burned it. Some of the British leaders decided the Spanish were to blame.

Col. John Palmer, who had been a member of Gov. Moore's party which raided St. Augustine in 1702, decided to get even with the Spanish.

He gathered a force and marched to the Indian village of Moosa, just north of St. Augustine. There, he attacked the Indians and won a major victory. The Spanish stayed in their fort and refused to come to the

King Philip of Spain invaded two countries and suddenly found Spain at war with four. Perhaps Spain could have conquered one or two countries, but four was more than she could handle.

15

Indians' aid. The Indians were so disappointed, they never forgave the Spanish.

With the Indian threat ended, Moore returned to the Carolinas but his retreat gave the Spanish little chance to relax.

FOUNDING OF GEORGIA

In 1732, James Oglethorpe, a British subject who hated the Spanish, secured a charter from England's king, granting him the right to establish a new colony, south of the Altamaha River. In January 1733, he arrived with the first of his settlers (some of whom were convicts) and founded Savannah, in what we now call Georgia.

This settlement finally stirred the Spanish to some kind of activity because they were certain this new colony meant new attacks on them.

From Cuba, a few additional soldiers were sent to St. Augustine. A few small boats also were sent to patrol the coastline. Two small outposts were established on the St. Johns River to help warn St. Augustine when the expected attack was launched.

During the next six years, these were the only improvements the Spanish made in their defenses and they simply were not enough.

OGLETHORPE ATTACKS

In 1739, in Europe, the mother countries of these two colonial settlements again went to war and, as before, it soon spread to the colonies.

The new war now gave Oglethorpe an excuse to attack.

In January 1740, he sent an expedition up the St. Johns and captured the two small forts — Pupa and Picolata — earlier established to protect St. Augustine. That cut off the route the few remaining friendly Indians might have used to come to St. Augustine's aid.

Four months later, in May 1740, he landed hundreds of additional soldiers on the beach 20 miles north of St. Augustine and took another small outpost there. The city now also was cut off from the north.

Then Oglethorpe laid siege to St. Augustine. For two months, the British invaders stayed near the city but their guns were not heavy enough to destroy the fort's walls. They tried to starve the people out.

In the meantime, word of the attack reached Cuba and the Spanish governor sent seven heavily armed ships to help. These were enough to make Oglethorpe retreat and he returned to Georgia.

James Oglethorpe founded Savannah with the help of debtors. Soon Georgia became known as a haven for those suffering from religious persecution. What other areas in the New World were religious sanctuaries?

The war in Europe stretched on for several more years and the Spanish and English colonies traded raids almost as long as their mother countries fought. Neither, however, could gain the upper hand and the fighting eventually died out.

For almost 20 years after that war ended, the two colonies lived in uneasy peace, neither trusting the other but neither strong enough to gain an advantage. Even an uneasy peace did not last between the French and British colonies and this, eventually, would affect the Spanish.

In July 1754, fighting between French and British colonials broke out in the Ohio River Valley. This was called the French and Indian War. Two years later, in 1756, it spread to Europe and became known there as the Seven Years' War.

Spain stayed neutral until late in that war and then decided to come to the aid of France.

Through all of this, Florida remained untouched. But, when England won the war, Spain paid the price of being on the losing side and Florida was part of the price she paid.

At the Peace of Paris, signed in 1763, Spain was required to give Florida to England in order to regain possession of Cuba and the Philippine Islands, which England had captured during the war.

France gave up all her claims west of the Mississippi River.

Thus, for the first time since the white man had come to North America, nearly 250 years before, Florida was in the hands of a country other than Spain.

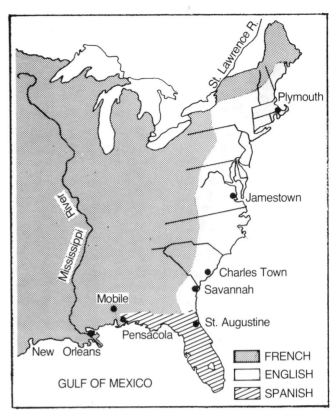

Active colonization efforts by England and France brought these countries closer to Spain's claims in Florida. This made Spain very uneasy. Which side did Spain eventually join?

Summary: Spain Loses Florida

While Spain had done little to strengthen her colonial holdings in Florida after establishing them, other European countries were more active.

The French moved inland along the Great Lakes, then south along the Mississippi River and soon became a real threat to the Spanish outpost at Pensacola.

The English colonies continued to grow along the Atlantic coast and moved steadily south toward Florida. Finally, in 1733, James Oglethorpe established the colony of Georgia which reached the St. Marys River and made the English an even more real threat to St. Augustine.

A series of European wars between the three mother countries of these colonial settlements led to fighting between the colonies and put the Spanish directly between two ever-growing powers.

In the last war of that series, Mother Spain stayed neutral until just before the war ended. Then, she chose wrong, deciding to join France in her fight against England. Although there was no fighting which involved Florida, when the war ended and the peace treaty was written, Florida was transferred to the British.

For the first time in 250 years, Spain no longer owned Florida.

Work Section

TRUE-FALSE

Answer the following questions true or false.
1. Robert Searles attack on St. Augustine caused very little damage.
2. The decision to build Castillo de San Marcos was a direct result of the Searles raid.
3. Castillo de San Marcos helped the defense of all Spanish settlements in Florida.
4. James Moore was governor of Carolina.
5. His raid against St. Augustine was the only one he staged in Florida.

6. Jaime Franck was governor of Pensacola.
7. European wars had no effect on the colonials in North America.
8. The French twice captured Pensacola.
9. The founding of Georgia brought a new threat to Spanish Florida.
10. Spain ceded Florida to England in order to regain possession of Cuba and the Philippine Islands.

MULTIPLE CHOICE

Only one of the following answers is correct. Mark the right one.

1. The first permanent English settlement in North America was
   a. Jamestown, Va.
   b. Plymouth, Mass.
   c. Roanoke Island
   d. None of the above
2. Castillo de San Marcos was capable of housing
   a. 50 people
   b. 500 people
   c. 1,500 people
   d. 5,000 people
3. The James Moore raid against St. Augustine was launched in
   a. 1650
   b. 1702
   c. 1585
   d. 1686
4. The first San Marcos de Apalache was captured by
   a. Pirates
   b. Indians
   c. French
   d. English
5. Georgia was founded by
   a. James Moore
   b. John Palmer
   c. Jean Baptiste le Moyne
   d. James Oglethorpe
6. In 1719, Pensacola was attacked by
   a. James Moore
   b. John Palmer
   c. Jean Baptiste le Moyne
   d. James Oglethorpe
7. The closest French settlement to Pensacola was
   a. Tallahassee
   b. San Marcos de Apalache
   c. Mobile
   d. New Orleans
8. The Spanish built two small forts at Pupa and
   a. St. Marks
   b. Jacksonville

c. Pensacola
d. Picolata

9. Spanish America was ceded to England by the peace treaty following
   a. King George's War
   b. The War of the Spanish Succession
   c. The Revolutionary War
   d. The Seven Years' War
10. Until England took control of Florida, it had belonged to Spain for
    a. 250 years
    b. 50 years
    c. 100 years
    d. 150 years

COMPLETION

Fill in the blanks in the following sentences with the correct word or phrase.

1. The Spanish decided to build the Castillo de San Marcos after the founding of
2. Raids of Spanish missions in the Apalachee area were conducted by
3. San Marcos de Apalache was located where the Wakulla and _____ rivers joined.
4. San Marcos de Apalache became an important
5. In 1718, four countries joined in an alliance against Spain. They were Austria, Holland, France and
6. _____ was attacked by a French fleet.
7. Col. John Palmer attacked the Indian Village of
8. In 1740, _____ attacked St. Augustine.
9. The Seven Years' War was known as the _____ War in North America.
10. The agreement which ceded Florida to England was called

SUGGESTED WORK PROJECTS

MAP SKILLS

A. Using a map of the United States, locate the following places and tell why they were important in Florida's history.
   1. Charles Town (Charleston, S.C.)
   2. Picolata
   3. Mobile
   4. New Orleans
   5. Havana, Cuba
   6. Savannah, Ga.
B. Have students outline a map of Florida and locate the three main forts — St. Augustine, San Marcos

and Pensacola — which existed at the time the territory was ceded to England. Have them discuss why there were no other Spanish settlements, other than the missions.

EXPLORING THE WORLD

A. Plan field trips, when possible, to the following sites
   1. Castillo de San Marcos
   2. San Marcos de Apalache
B. Obtain a piece of coquina rock and, using an encyclopedia (see limestone), explain how it is formed and why it is used for building.
C. Have students discuss why coquina would make an excellent material from which to build a fort.

Part III
The Changing Fate of Florida

THE TRANSFER

Spanish officials at St. Augustine were notified on March 16, 1763, that the mother country had agreed to the peace treaty which ended the Seven Years' War and that English officials would be arriving to replace them in Florida within a few weeks.

Military officers and some of the British troops which had captured Havana, Cuba, were to be transferred to Florida to begin British rule.

However, it was not until July 20, 1763 that the first of these troops arrived. On that date, Capt. John Hedges and four companies of the British 1st Regiment arrived in St. Augustine. The Spanish were prepared and turned the city over to them without argument.

Ten days later, the 9th Regiment, under command of Maj. Francis Ogilvie, also arrived from Havana. Ogilvie became military governor, to serve until a civilian governor could be appointed.

The transfer of Pensacola also was without problems. Lt. Col. Augustin Prevost arrived in that city on August 6, 1763, with members of the 3rd Battalion of the 60th Regiment. They, too, had sailed from Havana.

Transfer of the third Spanish settlement, San Marcos de Apalache, did not go so smoothly.

The Spanish had abandoned San Marcos de Apalache during the war but decided it should be re-occupied in order to make a formal transfer to the British.

Therefore, in August, they sent a small garrison under command of Capt. Don Bentura Diaz to the fort to await the British.

Augustin Prevost was the English representative at the transfer of Pensacola from the Spanish to the English. England's grand spoils at Pensacola consisted of about 100 huts, a few poorly-kept gardens, and the fort building.

Early in November, Capt. John Harries and a company of English troops arrived by boat. They stayed a week while Harries inspected the fort. The captain was hardly prepared for the isolation he found and, after his inspection, he sailed to Pensacola to protest occupation of the fort.

He explained it was so far from everything and there were so few sources of food and water, it would have to be stocked with at least four months' provisions in order for the garrison to survive. However, British authorities insisted he return and accept its transfer.

The ship was stocked with needed supplies and started on its return trip. However, it went aground and the supplies had to be thrown overboard to lighten the ship and free it. Harries again returned to Pensacola to restock and the official transfer was not completed until Feb. 20, 1764.

The Spanish, who had not planned for such an extended stay, nearly starved before they were relieved by the British.

The Changes

The British had not gained much in acquiring Florida.

St. Augustine, for example, was a town about a mile long and a quarter-mile wide, consisting of no more than 300 houses. The only major development was the fort — Castillo de San Marcos — a church and a hospital.

Pensacola offered even less. There were maybe 100 rude huts and a small fort, badly in need of repair.

San Marcos de Apalache offered only the fort.

When such reports reached England, the king concluded the new possession would have to be re-organized. On October 7, 1763, he issued a proclamation, dividing the new territory into East and West Florida.

Everything east of the Chattahoochee and Apalachicola rivers and north to the 31st parallel was to be known as East Florida. The territory west of those rivers, extending to the Mississippi River, was designated West Florida. St. Augustine was named the capital of East Florida, Pensacola the capital of West Florida.

Thus, England added its 14th and 15th colonies in North America.

English officials were determined to make the new colonies a source of trade. To do this, they realized they would have to develop friendship with the Indians and found a number of new settlements.

THE GOVERNORS

To accomplish the task of making friends with the Indians, British officials decided to appoint governors from among loyal British citizens who already were living in North America.

For East Florida, they selected James Grant. He had been in America for several years and had lived in South Carolina, where he had been active in nego-

The first governor of East Florida was James Grant. He knew that it would be to his advantage to have the Indians on the side of the English. He used conferences and gifts to settle disputes. Why were his methods more effective with the Indians than force?

tiations with the Cherokee Indians. He knew Indian affairs well and also was acquainted with many well-known South Carolina officials. Some of them he would appoint to help him govern East Florida.

He was an excellent choice and, when he arrived in August 1764, he was prepared and immediately went to work.

West Florida was not so fortunate.

Gov. George Johnstone had a questionable reputation and argued with the military leaders almost from the start. However, he also made attempts to make friends with the Indians.

Neither governor found much to govern. Most Spanish settlers left Florida for Cuba when the British arrived. A few stayed behind in St. Augustine to try to sell Spanish homes to the newcomers. A few British traders moved in to take over trade with the Indians.

In Pensacola, however, there was little more than the military who were stationed at the fort. The closest main settlement was 75 miles to the west, at Mobile. Most of the French settlers who had founded that city decided to remain, despite its transfer to the British.

NEW SETTLERS

Because so few people remained in the Floridas, British officials in England and those in the new colonies made strong efforts to attract new settlers.

Two types of land grants were made available.

One allowed grants of land up to 20,000 acres to any owner who would sponsor white families in the new colony. These grants also would allow up to 100 additional acres per person sent to live on the land.

The other type of grant was for individual family groups who would go on their own. This allowed 100 acres for the head of the family, 50 acres for each other family member and an option to buy 1,000 additional acres at a shilling per acre.

Many of both types of grants were claimed but very few were settled.

The main reason for this was that land also was available in the other colonies. Because these colonies were more settled, newcomers preferred to live there rather than in the isolation of Florida.

However, some major efforts were made to establish new colonies.

NEW SMYRNA

One of the most notable was New Smyrna. A group of high British officials in England obtained several of the 20,000-acre grants, all of which adjoined each other. They were located along the Atlantic coast, south of St. Augustine.

One of these officials was Dr. Andrew Turnbull and he was appointed manager of the new colony. The idea was to bring over people from countries along the Mediterranean Sea, who were familiar with tropical farming and tropical products, and produce similiar products at the new settlement. Products were to include such items as hemp, cotton and indigo.

In 1768, Turnbull arrived in Florida with about 1,500 people from Greece, Italy and the island of Minorca.

Gov. Grant had sent supplies to last about four months to the area. He had several large buildings constructed for the newcomers to live in, while they built their own homes.

Patrick Tonyn replaced Grant as governor of East Florida. During the American Revolution, Tonyn welcomed fleeing English Loyalists in St. Augustine.

Within a year, the new settlers had cleared several hundred acres of land along the Indian River and were producing corn, cotton, sugarcane, rice and indigo for export as well as other foods for their own use.

However, the colony was not producing enough to show a profit. Gov. Grant was unable to help because his resources for running East Florida were small. The owners in England refused to send more help because they felt they would never get their investment back.

Almost from the first, the colonists and Turnbull began having trouble. Because supplies were short and work was hard, many colonists died and efforts toward revolt began as early as the fall of 1768.

Conditions, unfortunately, got little better as the years passed. Then, in 1771, Grant returned to England, leaving Lt. Gov. John Moultrie in charge of East Florida. Moultrie and Turnbull had been enemies almost from the beginning of the New Smyrna settlement and, with Moultrie now in charge of East Florida, their differences became more marked.

In 1774, Patrick Tonyn arrived as the new governor and Moultrie immediately made charges that Turnbull was trying to cheat the New Smyrna partners who remained in England. He was successful and Tonyn arrested Turnbull, held a hearing for the New Smyrna settlers and gave them permission to abandon the colony and move to St. Augustine.

OTHER EFFORTS

While New Smyrna was the largest of the English attempts at further settlements in East Florida, there were smaller ones which were more successful.

Most of these were plantations, owned by government officials and operated by slave labor. Because they were owned by officials, they were able to make funds available with which to build roads to easily get their products to St. Augustine for export to Europe.

Therefore, while even these settlements were rather few in number, there were improvements made because of British policies and British money.

THE PRODUCTS

Most of the shipments from East Florida were such things as timber, lumber and timber products.

There were other products shipped, of course. By 1768, for example, there were even some oranges and orange juice shipped from St. Augustine.

In West Florida, however, such success was far more limited. Most settlers attracted to North America and bound for Florida, landed first at St. Augustine. Although it was not a large settlement, it was considerably bigger than Pensacola.

If settlers did decide to go on to West Florida, they were generally so disappointed in Pensacola, they elected to go on to Mobile and even to New Orleans.

As a result, Pensacola grew very little under British rule and British influence did not extend far west of that city. The French, for example, had stayed on in Mobile. Moreover, New Orleans had become a Spanish city under terms of the treaty of 1763.

Florida in the Revolution

All of these factors increased in importance on April 19, 1775. On that day, in the northern colony of Massachusetts, the shots were fired which signaled the start of the Revolutionary War.

Thirteen of England's fifteen North American colonies began the fight which would lead to the Declaration of Independence and the formation of the United States of America.

Why didn't East and West Florida also decide to seek independence?

There was some British worry they would but it proved to be unnecessary worry for several reasons.

First, both colonies were too new and too dependent upon England.

Second, both trade and taxes on the colonists were very limited. Therefore, there was not the base for disagreement such as existed in the older and more developed northern colonies.

Finally, England was paying the costs of governing the Floridas. As a result, neither colony could afford to become independent.

Despite these facts, England still worried. The main worry was the possibility that Spain, which still had colonial claims to the west of the Mississippi River, might decide to declare war against England. In that case, the Spanish who had gone to Cuba in 1763, might be a military threat, especially to the colony of West Florida.

There was also the possibility that soldiers from the revolting northern colonies might decide to attack East Florida.

SPANISH THREATS

The worry about Spanish threats soon proved to be real.

On New Year's Day 1777, Spanish authorities sent Bernardo de Galvez to New Orleans as the governor of Spanish claims along the Mississippi.

In June 1779, Spain decided to join France in her declaration of war against England. (England was now at war with the Colonies, France and Spain.)

Galvez was a well-known Spanish soldier and the declaration of war was all he needed to bring him into action.

Using soldiers who had come to New Orleans from Cuba, he began a march into West Florida. Within just a few weeks, he had captured most of the small settlements along the Gulf coast.

By February 1780, he arrived at Pensacola and laid seige to that city. The small garrison of British soldiers there managed to hold out for almost three months but, on May 8, 1780, they were forced to surrender.

All of West Florida was now back in Spanish control.

Bernardo de Galvez planned to take over Pensacola by means of the three-pronged attack from Havana, New Orleans, and Mobile.

WAR IN EAST FLORIDA

Attacks on East Florida by colonial soldiers from the north caused England fewer problems.

During 1776 and early as 1777, the Colonies made a few raids across the border separating Florida and Georgia but most raids were very small. British troops, stationed in St. Augustine, returned some of those raids but neither side mounted heavy attacks or did more than minor damage.

After 1777, the colonial soldiers were too busy fighting for their lives in their own colonies to be able to attack East Florida.

The main role played by East Florida, the larger of the two English Florida colonies, can be divided into two main parts.

The Castillo de San Marcos became a prison for French, Spanish and American sailors captured by the British and for some of the more prominent colonial leaders who also were captured.

Among the more prominent prisoners who were held in the Castillo were Arthur Middleton, Edward Rutledge and Thomas Heyward. All had been signers of the Declaration of Independence.

The other role played by East Florida was as a place of safety for colonists from the north who chose to remain loyal to England.

When it became apparent, early in 1782, that the northern colonies would win their freedom, the number of people fleeing to Florida for safety began to increase. Their arrival created a real problem for English authorities who had only limited housing and limited food supplies.

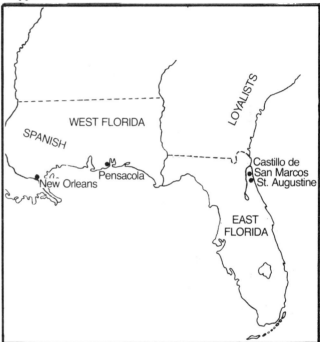
English-owned Florida had two problems during the American Revolution: an influx of Loyalists from the north, and Spanish raids from the west.

By the time the war ended in 1783, it was estimated more than 15,000 people had fled to St. Augustine. The food and housing situation in that city became very bad.

The biggest disappointment for these refugees came when terms of the new peace treaty were announced. Under those terms, England agreed to return Florida to the Spanish. Now, it was the fate of English settlers to have to leave their newest colonies.

In June 1784, the new Spanish governor — Manuel de Zespedes — arrived in St. Augustine and, by the end of 1785, the last of the British subjects had left.

Once again, Florida was in Spanish hands.

Summary: English Ownership and Loss

When England obtained Florida at the peace settlement of 1763, she found an almost undeveloped colony with very few people living in it. She immediately undertook changes in colonial policy, hoping to correct that condition.

She divided Florida into two colonies — East Florida and West Florida — and placed a crown-appointed governor over each. Through a system of grants, special efforts were made to get settlers to come to the Floridas. These efforts were only partly successful.

Most of the success was scored in East Florida, along the Atlantic coast line. During her 20 years of rule, England managed to make small improvements in strengthening that colony.

Special efforts were made to achieve friendship with the Indians in order to improve trade. As with settlers, this special effort was only partly successful.

When war with England's other colonies to the north started in 1775, Florida remained loyal to England and became a haven for loyalists who were forced to flee from the north.

The Castillo de San Marcos at St. Augustine served as an important prison for revolutionary leaders and for sailors captured during the war at sea.

As the war ground on, however, England soon found herself faced with European enemies again — particularly France and Spain. Spanish colonists from Cuba and New Orleans then launched attacks against West Florida and, when the war ended, England was forced to return Florida to Spain under terms of the new peace treaty.

Thus, the brief 20 years of English rule did not bring significant progress nor make significant changes. In 1783, the Spanish returned and two years later, the last of the British had left and Spanish rule resumed.

Work Section

TRUE-FALSE

Answer the following questions true or false.
1. Spanish officials were not notified in advance the British were taking over Florida.
2. English Capt. John Harries was not happy with the situation he found at San Marcos de Apalache.
3. England divided Florida into two colonies.
4. New Orleans was part of West Florida.
5. The largest attempt at colonization made by the British was at New Smyrna.
6. Most of Florida's exports under British rule were oranges and orange juice.
7. There was heavy fighting between colonial soldiers from northern English colonies and British soldiers in Florida during the Revolutionary War.
8. The Spanish recaptured the city of Pensacola from the British before the war ended.

MULTIPLE CHOICE

Only one of the following answers is correct. Mark the right one.
1. The first British troops to arrive in Florida were under command of
   a. Capt. John Harries
   b. Capt. John Hedges
   c. Maj. Francis Ogilvie
   d. Lt. Col. Augustin Prevost

2. The largest Spanish settlement the British found was
   a. San Marcos de Apalache
   b. Mobile
   c. St. Augustine
   d. Pensacola
3. The first permanent governor of East Florida was
   a. Maj. Francis Ogilvie
   b. John Moultrie
   c. George Johnstone
   d. James Grant

4. England offered grants to attract new settlers. There were
   a. Three kinds
   b. Four kinds
   c. Five kinds
   d. None of the above
5. The manager of the New Smyrna colony was
   a. Dr. Andrew Turnbull
   b. Maj. Francis Ogilvie
   c. James Grant
   d. Capt. John Harries

6. The governor who arrested Turnbull was
   a. Patrick Tonyn
   b. John Moultrie
   c. Don Bentura Diaz
   d. None of the above

7. The Spanish leader who recaptured Pensacola was
   a. Don Bentura Diaz
   b. Pedro Menendez de Aviles
   c. Bernardo de Galvez
   d. None of the above
8. Three signers of the Declaration of Independence was imprisoned in St. Augustine's Castillo de San Marcos. They were Arthur Middleton, Edward Rutledge and
   a. James Grant
   b. Thomas Heyward
   c. John Harries
   d. George Johnstone

COMPLETION

Fill in the blank in the following sentences with the correct word or phrase.
1. The treaty by which Spain transferred Florida to the British followed the
2. There were about   houses in St. Augustine when the British occupied that city.
3. The   and   rivers were the dividing line between East and West Florida.
4. One type of land grant offered by the British allowed owners to claim up to   acres.
5. Most of the settlers who came to New Smyrna were from

6. The main products shipped from Florida were
7. The Spanish launched their attack against West Florida from
8. The   were a group of people who fled to Florida for safety from the 13 northern colonies.

SUGGESTED WORK PROJECTS

1. Using a map, locate the following places and tell why they were important in Florida's history.
   a. New Smyrna
   b. Mobile
   c. New Orleans
   d. Pensacola
   e. St. Augustine
   f. The Chattahoochee and Apalachicola rivers
2. Have a group of class members do a study and make a presentation on hemp and its uses.
3. Have another group do a similar project on indigo.
4. Where possible, plan field trips to the following sites:
   a. St. Augustine and Castillo de San Marcos
   b. Pensacola
   c. San Marcos de Apalache (St. Marks)
5. Have a group of students do a study and make a presentation on the type of timber products which were important in the days of sailing ships.

Part IV

Florida
Under Spanish Rule

SPAIN'S PROBLEMS

When Vincente Manuel de Zespedes returned to St. Augustine in 1784 to once again govern Florida for Spain, he brought with him a force of about 500 soldiers. Many Spanish civilians who had lived in Florida before it became British also returned.

But, Spain was faced with a much different situation than that which had existed when she lost Florida to England 20 years earlier.

Spain was much weaker internationally. Much of her world influence had disappeared and two wars had cost her a great deal of her national wealth.

To the north of Florida, instead of a group of British colonies, Spain now faced a new nation, the United States. It was a nation fresh from gaining its independence from one of the world's most powerful countries, England.

Within the boundaries of Florida, Spain also faced problems — problems which a force of 500 soldiers would not be able to solve. For example, many British and loyalist adventurers had stayed on. Most had grown wealthy through trade with the Indians and they were determined to continue that wealth through trade. Others simply disliked Spain and were just as determined to make trouble for that nation.

Troubles Begin Early

Under terms of the peace treaty, the British had until mid-1785 to leave Florida. Gov. Patrick Tonyn was to be allowed to stay to protect British interests until all Englishmen had left.

Tonyn and Zespedes often did not agree on policies which the Spanish wanted to enforce. Moreover, most loyalists who had fled to Florida from the Carolina and Georgia colonies resented the return of Florida to Spain and were determined to make trouble.

DANIEL McGIRT

One of the most determined of these was Daniel McGirt, a loyalist who had come to Florida from the Carolinas.

McGirt began raiding British plantations along the St. Johns River and soon had Tonyn and Zespedes arguing about who should handle his case when he would

be captured.

After a number of destructive raids, McGirt and several of his band were captured. Tonyn insisted they be tried in British courts but, instead Zespedes sent them off to Havana. The act created more hard feelings between the two governors.

Several times, McGirt managed to return to Florida before he eventually was sent to the Bahamas and passed completely from the Florida scene.

But, his example showed the way for others and, even after the British left in November 1785, confusion continued to haunt Spanish rule.

INDIAN PROBLEMS

During their 20-year stay, the British had built a sound trade with both Florida Indians and those Indians across the border in what was now the United States. The Spanish had never had the same degree of success.

With British departure, most Indians began to look to the United States for their main source of trade.

The Spanish, however, wishing to keep the Indians from becoming friendly with this new nation, decided to allow Panton Leslie and Co., a British trading company, to remain in Florida. By granting the company a monopoly in Indian trade, they felt the Indians would be more friendly toward the Spanish.

The Indians, on the other hand, were torn between several possibilities. They knew trade with the former British colonies — now the U.S. — would be to their benefit. They also realized, however, that the country would probably do everything in its power to further expand its national boundaries. That meant they would try to acquire Florida and they would push their frontiers westward; these two actions would cost the Indians land which was traditionally theirs.

The Indians also knew, from long experience, trade with the Spanish hardly would be to their benefit.

With that in mind, they generally favored continued trade with Panton Leslie. That attitude paved the way for one of their own tribal members to become an outstanding figure in relations among Spain, England and the U.S. and in the fate of Florida.

ALEXANDER McGILLIVRAY

One of the most successful white traders in the Carolinas and Georgia during the closing years of British colonial rule was a Scot — Lachlan McGillivray. During the years of his success, he married a Creek Indian princess and they had a son they named Alexander McGillivray.

When the Revolutionary War broke out in 1775, the elder McGillivray, loyal to the British crown, fled to Scotland, leaving more than $100,000 in property behind.

More important to the Florida story, he also left his son behind. The young man was raised in Savannah, Ga., and Charleston, S.C., attending the finest schools in those cities. He also became very familiar with Indian ways as he spent long periods with the Creeks, learning their ways. He was trained for leadership in the tribe because his mother was an Indian princess.

By 1784, when he was only 25 years old, Alexander McGillivray had become a power in his own right. His father had known the leaders of Panton Leslie, thus the son was familiar with their trading methods. His education in white schools had provided him with a sound basis in the white man's way of life. His association and training with the Indians rounded out his qualifications.

He soon had become symbolic chief of more than 45,000 Indians — Creeks, Chickasaws, Choctaws and Seminoles — an all-important factor in the situation which was developing in Florida and along its borders.

McGILLIVRAY'S METHODS

With such influence, the British, through Panton Leslie, made him their official contact with all Indians. He would distribute gifts and arms to his subjects. The British Army also made him a colonel.

The same year, McGillivray met with Spanish officials in Pensacola. He signed a treaty on behalf of the Indians which promised Spanish protection for the Indians and more arms and ammunition.

In succeeding years, as the power of the United States became more evident, McGillivray began dealing with that new nation, as well. In 1790, President George Washington asked the Indian leader to come to New York to try to work out an agreement with the United States. Together, Washington and McGillvray signed the Treaty of New York. Under its terms, the Indians agreed to keep all foreign traders out of land they controlled and McGillivray pleged his people would recognize the U.S. again, there was personal profit--a pension from the new goverment.

Thus, by 1790, McGillivray was on the payroll of three nations — England, Spain and the U.S., proving once again the importance all of them attached to Indian relations along the Florida-United States border.

To his credit, while he lived, McGillivray kept peace along that border. But, when the young chief died in 1793, a new, less-peaceable adventurer entered the picture.

WILLIAM AUGUSTUS BOWLES

William Augustus Bowles came to Florida as a 15-year-old ensign in a Maryland loyalist regiment. This regiment had been assigned to duty in Pensacola during the Revolutionary War.

When the war ended, like McGillivray's father, he married an Indian girl and then chose to live with the Indians.

Jealous of McGillivray's success, he planned and plotted to become equally as influential. But, it was not until 1788 that he began to be recognized by others. In that year, sponsored by a number of other dissatisfied loyalists who had been forced to leave Florida, he met Alexander McGillivray on their behalf.

He offered to supply McGillivray's tribesmen with arms and ammunition but only if they would use them to make war upon the Georgia frontier.

The Indian chief was opposed to the Georgians pushing westward but he did not want open warfare and refused Bowles' offer.

That wasn't enough to stop Bowles.

He went to the Bahama Islands, collected a force of about 30 men and all of the arms and ammunition he could transport to Florida. His group landed near the mouth of the Indian River, planning to attack the Spanish outpost on Lake George.

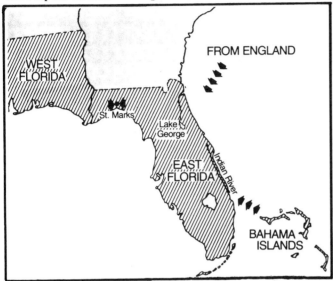

Ambitious William Bowles plotted several times to become a central figure in Florida history. He succeeded, but not in the way he intended.

His plan was to take the outpost, fortify it, arm the Indians in the area and use it as a base for attacks on the Spanish. However, most of his followers deserted him and he was forced to turn elsewhere to carry out his plan.

He decided the small Spanish fort at St. Marks would be easier to attack. But, even the small number of soldiers there was great enough to withstand the attack and Bowles was captured. He was taken to Havana and put into prison there. Later the Spanish transferred him to Africa but he escaped and made his way to England.

There, he managed to talk other dissatisfied former Florida residents into supporting another try at the overthrow of Spanish rule in Florida.

Again, his force was small and, though he landed in Florida, he soon was captured and returned to Cuba. There, he died in prison in 1803.

TREATY OF SAN ILDEFONSO

Spain and the United States were also torn by a dispute about land ownership in the early years after Spain regained Florida.

During the 20 years of British rule there, that country had claimed a northern Florida boundary of 32 degrees, 30 minutes. The colonies did not protest because all of the land belonged to England.

When the area was returned to Spain, however, that claim did cause trouble. The new United States asserted the northern boundary had always been 31 degrees.

The disagreement was an almost constant source of tension between the two countries. Finally, in 1795, Spain bowed to U.S. demands for a settlement and agreed to the 31st degree as the border. The agreement was sealed in the Treaty of San Ildefonso.

There were few Spanish forces in the disputed area but it was several months before they were pulled back behind the newly agreed-upon line. The slowness with which they moved made frontiersmen along the border angry.

New tensions developed. Georgians, who were anxious to move their borders westward, complained to members of Congress. Others, less ready to accept that way of action, decided to take matters into their own hands.

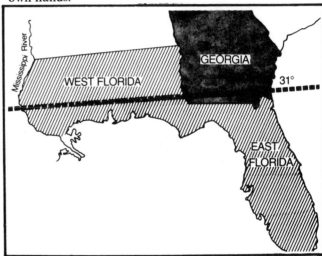

The Treaty of San Ildefonso established the Georgia-Florida border. It also signified Spain's acknowledgement of her lessening power in the New World.

Arming themselves, they decided to attack the Spanish and force them to move.

The first trouble came in the area near the city now known as Baton Rouge, La. A group of pioneers attacked the Spanish headquarters there, forced the Spanish governor to flee and declared the whole of West Florida free and independent of Spain.

When word of that revolt reached Georgia, frontiersmen there again appealed to Congress. They claimed that Englishmen who had stayed in Florida were arming both Indians and runaway black slaves, encouraging them to make raids into territory which properly belonged to Georgia.

Finally, in 1811, Congress acted. It authorized the President to occupy Florida — peacefully, if possible, but by force, if necessary — in order to combat these raids.

With that kind of encouragement, the Georgians decided not to wait for authorized U.S. troops but to move on their own.

George Mathews, a former governor of Georgia, raised a force and marched into Florida. He met little resistance and led his men all the way to St. Augustine but was unable to force the Spanish to deal with him.

THE WAR OF 1812

It looked as if a stalemate had occurred but a dangerous one with an unauthorized force of Americans besieging the Spanish capital on Spanish soil.

Then, on June 18, 1812, the United States declared war on England.

That put Florida in a new light. Although it was Spanish, as former owners, the English were quite familiar with the territory. It became obvious they might try to use it as a base from which to attack the least populated part of the new nation.

Again, Georgians were quick to act. Using war as an excuse, they began concentrated raids all along the Florida border.

Spanish Gov. Sebastian Kindelan — already short of soldiers — was forced to turn to Indians in Florida and runaway slaves in order to get enough men together to protect his territory from a full-scale invasion.

The two sides faced each other, armed and ready. However, neither was strong enough to defeat the other and the result was a series of small and inconclusive fights all along the common border.

In the West

Meanwhile, the British were aware that the western end of that same frontier would be easier to attack. With that goal, they landed men and supplies in West Florida. Their aim was to arm the Indians and attack that western frontier.

By 1813, they were ready and, later the same year, a group of Indians attacked the United States' Fort Mims, an isolated outpost where the Alabama and Tombigbee rivers joined in West Florida.

Several hundred Americans were killed in the attack.

Word of the defeat quickly spread throughout the United States and reaction was immediate.

In Tennessee, Gen. Andrew Jackson quickly raised a force of volunteers and prepared to strike back. He marched on an Indian stronghold at Horseshoe Bend, killing many of the Indians and driving the rest south toward Florida.

A victorious Jackson now sought more action. When word reached him the British had landed a group of marines at Pensacola — without protest from the Spanish — and were forming a new army of blacks and Indians, Jackson decided that would be his next target.

THE WILDERNESS FORT

Without approval from President Madison for the invasion of Florida, he struck at Pensacola. The move took the British by surprise and they were forced to flee.

Loading their troops on transports, they sailed east as far as the Apalachicola River. There, they landed and began gathering a new force of blacks and Indians. About 15 miles inland, up the river, they built a fort named Gadsden and turned it over to this new "army."

Meanwhile, the war had ended.

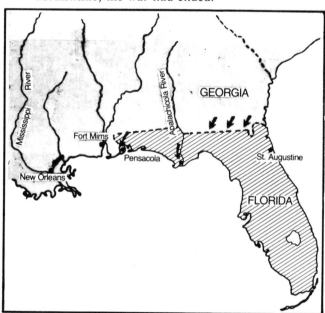

The War of 1812 gave Georgians an excuse to attack Spanish-owned Florida. Florida became a skirmish area between English and American forces. Weakened Spain was unable to stop these countries from fighting in Florida.

Not knowing that, Jackson marched from Pensacola to New Orleans and inflicted a major defeat on the British — a battle that was actually fought after the war was over.

Still determined to drive the British from Florida, he wrote the Spanish governor in Pensacola and told him he would have to see that the British-sponsored fort on the Apalachicola River was closed or Jackson himself would bring American soldiers back to Florida and force its closing.

The Spanish chose to ignore the demand. Jackson ordered an attack and, in July 1816, Americans came downriver from Georgia, shelled the fort, blew it up and killed most of those manning the fort.

Now, the U.S. government issued a new demand that Spain either police Florida to keep peace along the border or cede it to the United States.

Back in the East

Meanwhile, action shifted elsewhere along the border. Unfortunately for the Spanish, the British and Americans were not the only ones aware of Spanish weaknesses in Florida.

In June 1817, a Scots trader — George McGregor — landed a force on Amelia Island, near the Atlantic border between Georgia and Florida.

McGregor had fought with Simon Bolivar in Venezuela, where the battle to also remove the Spanish from rule was increasing in strength. McGregor's group established an armed camp and declared the island independent of Spanish rule.

Spanish soldiers, who had maintained an outpost there, fled without a fight. McGregor raised what he called the Green Flag of Florida, a St. George Cross in green on a white field.

For several weeks, the Spanish made half-hearted efforts to oust McGregor without success.

In the meantime, Luis Aury, one of Mexico's most famous pirates, decided that he, too, would launch an attack on Amelia Island. In September 1817, he landed another group, chased McGregor's forces away and raised yet another flag — that of the Republic of Mexico.

Aury began trading in pirate goods, launched a huge slave trade and, once again, brought the United States into the dispute.

In December 1817, President James Monroe sent a naval squadron to the island, landed a force of 200 Marines and forced Aury to flee. He then sent word to Spain that U.S. troops would hold the island in protective custody.

As it turned out, those troops would remain there until Spain sold Florida to the U.S.

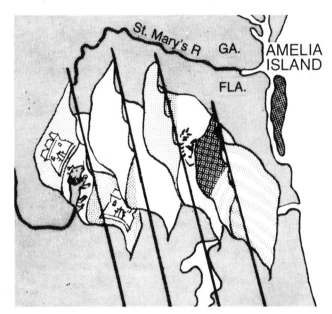

Amelia Island was a good example of the constantly changing land ownerships in Florida. During 1817, the island had a succession of four different flags flying over it.

MORE TROUBLES WITH THE BRITISH

That brought peace to the eastern shore but now the British re-entered the picture in Florida. Led by the same George McGregor who had invaded Amelia Island, a group of British traders decided to establish a new trading post at St. Marks.

Again, the aim was to arm the Indians and encourage them to attack the U.S. frontier.

Early in December 1817, President Monroe gave Gen. Edmund Gaines permission to attack the Indians to forestall the British efforts. The President sent a copy of his order to Gen. Jackson. The only restriction he placed on their action was they were not to attack the Indians if they sought shelter in a Spanish-held fort.

Such a restriction meant little to Jackson. He decided he would take personal charge of the fight against the Indians.

By March 1818, Jackson arrived at the Florida-Georgia border with a force of 800 men of the regular Army, 900 Georgia volunteers and 300 friendly Indians. At their head, he marched into Florida.

ARBUTHNOT-AMBRISTER AFFAIR

When McGregor had accepted his new assignment at the new trading post at St. Mark's, he had hired two British citizens to help him in his task of stirring up the Indians.

Robert Christie Ambrister was a former British officer who had elected to stay in Florida when Spain regained control of that area. Alexander Arbuthnot was a British trader of questionable reputation.

Tales and examples of their exploits reached Jackson long before he arrived at St. Marks and the two men were high on his enemies' list.

Shortly after he took over the fort at St. Marks, where Arbuthnot conducted much of his trade, word reached him that the Englishman was scheduled to arrive with a new load of arms for the Indians.

In anticipation, he decided to fly the English flag over the fort.

Within a couple of days, Arbuthnot's ship came sailing up the river. Jackson allowed him to dock, then took him, his crew and his cargo into custody.

Several days later, Ambrister and several members of his gang, who had been making contacts with the Indians, also stumbled into St. Marks.

Jackson also placed them under arrest.

Late in April, the general convened a court martial. It tried both men for their parts in the Indian raids. They were found guilty.

On April 29, Ambrister was shot by a firing squad. The same day, Arbuthnot was hung from a yardarm of his own ship.

Jackson then departed St. Marks to return to Georgia, certain that troubles with the Indians had ended.

However, when he arrived in Georgia, he was told more Indians were gathering in Pensacola and the Spanish there were interfering with supplies intended for shipment upriver to U.S. forts in Georgia.

Jackson raised yet another force, marched into Spanish Pensacola and took charge of that city.

END OF SPANISH RULE

Jackson's numerous exploits set off a huge debate in the United States Congress. His opponents argued he had no right to invade Florida, much less sentence two British subjects to death.

His supporters argued invasion of Florida was necessary to prevent Indians from raiding U.S. territory.

The argument lasted all summer before President Monroe finally decided to return the captured forts to the Spanish.

However, with their return, negotiations were opened to allow the U.S. to purchase the territory.

On Feb. 22, 1819, a treaty finally was signed. In it,

President Monroe (left) authorized Gaines to attack Florida's Indians so that British efforts might be slowed. Jackson (right) interpreted these orders to authorize him to attack the Spaniards in Florida.

the U.S. purchased Florida by assuming Spanish debts to U.S. citizens in the amount of approximately $5-million. In return, the U.S. surrendered any claim to Spanish territory west of the Sabine River, the area we now know as Texas.

Two days later, the Congress ratified the treaty.

The Spanish were less willing to act and another two years passed before that nation also agreed to the pact.

Finally, on Feb. 22, 1821, the Adams-Onis Treaty (named for the U.S. Secretary of State, and the Spanish Ambassador to the U.S.) was ratified. It was agreed the territory would be transferred to United States control later the same year.

JACKSON AS GOVERNOR

Even before the treaty was published, President Monroe turned to the American he felt was most familiar with Florida to become governor for the territory — Andrew Jackson.

He had talked to Jackson as early as 1819, when the Adams-Onis treaty first was proposed, but the general declined the offer. In January 1821, he again wrote Jackson, renewing the offer and, this time, the general reluctantly accepted.

Jackson left his home in Nashville, Tenn., and proceeded as far as Mobile. There, he waited until he was certain the Spanish had received instructions to leave.

On the morning of July 17, 1821, Jackson rode into Pensacola, met with Spanish governor Jose Callava and participated in a formal ceremony making Florida a territory of the United States.

A week before that, July 10, 1821, similar ceremonies were observed in St. Augustine, where Col. Robert Butler represented Jackson.

A third transfer ceremony was conducted at St. Marks on July 19, 1821, but that exchange was much less formal than the other two.

Jackson, who had not wanted the assignment in Florida, was determined to complete it as quickly as possible.

One of his first acts was to proclaim Florida a single territory. To simplify the problem of government, he divided it into two counties — Escambia and St. Johns. The former took in all the territory west of the Suwannee River and the latter everything east of that line.

He established government by executive order, providing 10 justices of the peace for each county and continuing the Spanish system of mayor and aldermen

for city governments in Pensacola and St. Augustine, the county seats.

Jackson divided Florida into two counties. He remained until a territorial government could be set up.

President Monroe appointed the most important officials for the new territory. Because he did not consult Jackson on those appointments, the governor became even more unhappy with his task.

Finally, on Oct. 5, 1821, Jackson wrote the President, telling him he considered his mission accomplished and he would now return to Tennessee. He intended, he said, not to return to Florida unless the public good demanded it.

FLORIDA AS A TERRITORY

On March 30, 1822, the Congress of the United States created a territorial government for Florida. It followed the blueprint laid down in the Northwest Ordinance of 1787, which provided for simple steps toward self-government and eventual statehood.

Included in the provisions were positions of governor, a secretary of state and a 13-man legislative council.

William Pope Duval was appointed to fill the office of governor. A native of Virginia, Duval went to the Kentucky frontier when only 14 years old and was admitted to the bar when only 19.

His contributions to that territory were great enough to win him election to the Congress of the United States from Kentucky in 1813. He had come to Florida as a territorial judge during Jackson's short term.

Before his years of office ended, he would be governor for 12 years and Florida would move well down the road toward statehood.

Summary: Spain Loses Florida [Again]

The second period of Spanish rule in Florida was short but marked with almost constant tensions.

The period was marred by border wars, illegal invasions and Spanish inability to control its territory.

That inability finally led President James Monroe to approve of U.S. takeovers of areas in Florida to assure the safety of its own borders and, finally, to negotiations leading to the purchase of Florida from Spain.

That purchase was finally completed in 1821 and the task now turned to preparing Florida, first, to become a territory of the U.S. and, second, to start it down the road to eventual statehood.

Work Section

TRUE-FALSE

Answer the following questions, true or false.
1. Spanish governor Vincente Manuel de Zespedes and British governor Patrick Tonyn worked well together in the transfer of Florida.
2. Daniel McGirt was a Spanish nobleman.
3. Panton Leslie was an English trading company.
4. Alexander McGillivray was a full-blooded Indian.
5. George Washington never met Alexander McGillivray.
6. William Augustus Bowles died in prison.
7. Gen. Jackson led U.S. troops at the Battle of Horseshoe Bend.
8. The Green Cross of Florida was a Spanish flag.
9. Alexander Arbuthnot was hanged.
10. Andrew Jackson was the first governor of Florida.

MULTIPLE CHOICE

Only one of the following answers is correct. Mark the right one.

1. England controlled Florida for
   a. 20 years
   b. 10 years
   c. 50 years
   d. 5 years

2. The Spanish granted a trading monopoly with the Indians to
   a. Daniel McGirt
   b. Patrick Tonyn
   c. Panton Leslie
   d. none of the above

3. Alexander McGillivray was
   a. The son of a Scot trader
   b. The son of an Indian princess
   c. Most important Indian chief on the frontier
   d. All of the above

4. The Treaty of San Ildefonso
   a. Ceded Florida to the United States
   b. Established the border line between Florida and the U.S.
   c. Made trade between the U.S. and Florida legal
   d. Made peace between the U.S. and the Indians

5. The War of 1812
   a. Was between the U.S. and England
   b. Was between Spain and the U.S.
   c. Was fought entirely in Florida
   d. Concerned none of these countries

6. The British established a fort on the Apalachicola River
   a. Called Ft. Tonyn
   b. For Indians and runaway slaves
   c. Called St. Marks
   d. Manned only by British soldiers

7. Amelia Island was invaded by
   a. George McGregor
   b. Luis Aury
   c. The U.S. Marines
   d. All of the above

8. Robert Christie Ambrister was
   a. British governor of Florida
   b. Spanish governor of Florida
   c. A former British officer
   d. Commanding officer of St. Marks

9. The Adams-Onis Treaty
   a. Allowed the U.S. to purchase Florida
   b. Set the boundary line between Florida and the U.S.
   c. Ceded Texas to the U.S.
   d. Gave Spain sole possession of Florida

10. President of the U.S. when Florida became part of that country was
    a. George Washington
    b. James Madison
    c. Andrew Jackson
    d. James Monroe

COMPLETION

Fill in the blank in the following sentences with the correct word or phrase.
1. Alexander McGillivray's mother was
2. William Augustus Bowles came to Florida during
3. Bowles escaped from the Spanish after he was taken to
4. Luis Aury was a famous
5. The _____ chased Aury off Amelia Island.
6. Ambrister died

36

7. Jackson accepted the transfer of Pensacola from

8.   represented the U.S. during the transfer at St. Augustine

9. William Pope Duval came to Florida as

10. Congress created a territorial government for Florida on

SUGGESTED WORK PROJECTS

1. Using a map, locate the following places and tell why they were important in Florida's history during the period discussed in this chapter.

    a. Amelia Island
    b. Pensacola
    c. St. Marks
    d. Ft. Gadsden

2. If possible, take class on a field trip to Ft. Gadsden State Park.

Part V
Florida Gains Statehood

SELECTION OF A CAPITAL

When Florida became a territory of the United States, it was governed by a legislative council. The council was made up of a governor and 13 delegates, all appointed by the President of the United States.

Representatives appointed to that council were drawn from the only two major population centers of the territory — Pensacola and St. Augustine. In order for the members to meet, it meant half of them had to travel long distances through wilderness or by water routes to gather with the others.

In 1822, the first meeting of the council was scheduled to be held in Pensacola. Four members of the St. Augustine group spent more than two weeks traveling to Pensacola by ship. A fifth lost his life when the ship on which he sailed was wrecked in a storm.

In order to make the annual meeting fair to all, it was decided the 1823 meeting would be held in St. Augustine. The same sort of travel problems occurred again and one of the acts of the 1823 council was to appoint a committee to find a suitable site for a permanent capital some place midway between the two cities.

John Lee Williams of Pensacola and Dr. William H. Simmons of St. Augustine were appointed by Gov. William Duval to find that site. In October 1823, they met in St. Marks, explored central Florida and settled upon the area we now call Tallahassee for the site of the new capital.

On March 4, 1824, Governor Duval proclaimed it the state capital and, in November 1824, the legislative council met there for the first time. The capital has remained in Tallahassee ever since. The name, inciden-

William Pope Duval was a judge of East Florida before he became its first territorial governor.

tally, is taken from a Cherokee Indian word meaning "old town".

CHANGES IN GOVERNMENT

During the next two years, the appointed council went about the business of establishing a more workable government within the territory. Among other things, it created 11 new counties. In 1826, with approval of the Congress of the United States, the council became an elected body, with voters choosing one representative from each of the 13 counties. The governor remained appointive and Duval continued in that position.

Florida also was granted the right to elect a delegate to the U.S. House of Representatives to assist the national government in development within the new territory. He was charged with three main duties: land disposal, internal improvements and Indian affairs. Richard Keith Call was the first delegate elected.

LAND CLAIMS

When the United States purchased Florida from Spain, it agreed to honor land grants which had been made before Jan. 24, 1818. Many of these had originated during the period Florida was owned by England, and others during the second period of Spanish rule. Records were unclear and it finally became necessary to appoint a commission of three members to come to Florida and decide which land grants would be honored. Many claims were settled in the courts only after long years of debate.

INTERNAL IMPROVEMENTS

The United States government appointed Col. Robert Butler as surveyor-general for the territory. It was his job to layout the territory and help to open it to new settlers.

This would provide a major step forward for expansion of Florida but most agreed the most necessary act would be to attain statehood. That subject, however, helped to divide the feelings of people already in the territory.

In the United States, the debate over slavery already was growing, causing a division between northern and southern states. Many in Florida wanted it to remain a territory until such time as the population had grown large enough to permit creation of two states, which would give the south an advantage in number of states. Others wanted statehood as soon as possible in order to push development of the new state with added support from the federal government.

Col. Butler served as an aide to Andrew Jackson before Butler was appointed surveyor-general. This photo was taken several years before his death in 1860.

The Indian Situation

As the number of settlers pouring into Florida increased, problems with the Indians also grew.

When the British and Spanish had ruled Florida, they had left almost the whole of middle Florida to the Indians. During the closing years of Spanish rule, border troubles with the United States had forced many Indians across the line into Florida where they felt they would enjoy a greater degree of freedom.

Now, the newly-arrived whites in Florida felt the Indians were in the way, blocking lands which the whites wanted. As a result, pressures began to mount to remove the Indians from Florida, sending them westward to Indian Territory.

The Indians, on the other hand, felt the lands they had occupied for the past 10,000 years were rightfully theirs. They were determined to resist removal, even to the point of fighting, if necessary.

At first, attempts were made to reach agreement by treaty. The first formal agreement was called the Treaty of Moultrie Creek, reached at a site of that name, about five miles south of St. Augustine.

It was approved by the U.S. Congress on Dec. 23, 1823 and set aside about four-million acres of land as a reservation for the Indians. The reservation boundaries extended from just above Charlotte Harbor on the south to just below Ocala on the north.

No one was truly satisfied with this arrangement. The Indians were slow to begin their move onto reservation lands and the whites continued to press for complete removal of the Indians from Florida.

Several more important meetings were held in an attempt to get the Indians to agree to move to Indian Territory, which we now know as Oklahoma. Finally, in 1832, a new meeting was called at Payne's Landing on the Oklawaha River.

James Gadsden, who had negotiated the Treaty of Moultrie Creek, again represented the United States. This time, however, only a few Indian chiefs were present. After much talk, these few agreed to migrate. However, those who had refused to attend also refused to comply with the agreement.

SECOND SEMINOLE WAR

In the weeks that followed, Gen. Wiley Thompson, who was serving as Indian agent, talked with many of those who had not signed the Payne's Landing agreement and warned them they would either have to go peacefully or they eventually would be removed by force. He set Jan. 1, 1836, as the date for removal to begin.

Many Indians reluctantly decided they had no choice. Others decided to resist. Among the resisters was Osceola, who became one of the most famous Indian leaders in Florida history.

Osceola rallied the Indians who did not want to leave Florida and, in December 1835, as others had begun to gather in Tampa preparatory to leaving, the hostile Indians struck.

A number of small fights broke out as early as Dec. 17, 1835, but the war began in earnest on Dec. 28, 1835.

On that day, Gen. Thompson and a fellow officer were killed by Indians as they walked outside the stockade at Ft. King, near today's city of Ocala.

Records say that Osceola died from quinsy (sore throat) and malaria. Before Florida was developed and drained, malaria was a risk people living in Florida had to take. Why did malaria decrease when Florida was drained?

The same day Thompson was killed, Maj. Francis Dade and two companies of soldiers, marching from Ft. Brooke to Ft. King, were ambushed near the small town of Bushnell and 108 soldiers were killed in the attack. Only three managed to escape.

The Second Seminole War was underway. Fighting would continue in many parts of Florida until 1842 and hundreds of lives would be lost on both sides. One of those who would die as a result of the war was Osceola.

OSCEOLA

Blame for most of the major incidents which occurred during the first part of the Second Seminole War was placed at the door of the great leader Osceola. If he had participated in all of the events he was blamed for, he indeed would have been a superman.

Strangely, although he was an Indian, Osceola was not a Seminole Indian. Most people still do not agree on his background. Generally, it is believed he was the son of a white man and a Creek Indian woman. Others contend he was full-blooded Indian. But, all agree he was not of the Seminole tribe, but belonged to the Red Stick group of the Upper Creek tribe, one of those which had fled from the Georgia-Alabama area.

Regardless, he became an important leader — although never a chief — in the war, which soon reached proportions unexpected by the whites in Florida.

Fighting broke out along all of the areas in which white men had settled and soon reached central Florida to the east coast and down as far south as Key Biscayne and the Everglades. One of the most important battles occurred in the Everglades on Christmas Day, 1837.

In September 1837, Thomas Jesup, the Army commander, was told a group of Indians were in camp near St. Augustine. He surprised the group and captured them. In the number taken was one of the principal chiefs, King Philip. They were taken to St. Augustine and placed in the prison there, known as Ft. Marion. King Philip asked that members of his family be allowed to come to the prison to stay with him.

One of those was his son Coacoochee, called Wild Cat by the whites. Coacoochee offered to become messenger to Osceola, who was in the neighborhood. Gen. Joseph Hernandez was sent by Gen. Jesup to meet with Osceola under a flag of truce so they could talk about ending the war.

The meeting was arranged for Oct. 21, 1837. Hernandez surrounded the meeting place with armed soldiers and, when Osceola came in to talk, he captured him.

In December, Osceola and almost 200 members of his band were transferred to Ft. Moultrie, S.C., and, in

January 1838, Osceola died there while in captivity. He was only 34 years old.

But, the capture of King Philip and Osceola did not end the war as had been expected. Other bands simply moved farther south, fighting as they went.

FIRST CONSTITUTION

In spite of that continued fighting, officials decided the time had come for the territory to draw up a constitution and submit it in an effort to become a state.

In December 1838, Richard Keith Call, Florida's third territorial governor, called a constitutional convention to sit in the city of St. Joseph.

Richard Call was first brought to Florida by Andrew Jackson, before Jackson departed in 1822. As territorial governor, Call arranged for the first Constitutional Convention.

A total of 56 delegates, 20 from East and Middle Florida and 16 from West Florida, worked for 34 consecutive days, under the watchful eye of Convention Chairman Robert Raymond Reid, to prepare the document under which Florida eventually would enter as a member of the United States.

Forty-nine of the representatives had been born in 26 other states of the union, indicating the speed with which newcomers were arriving in Florida. Four other members had been born in foreign countries and only three were native Floridians.

A great many of them would be important in Florida's history.

Included in that number were former territorial governor William Duval and Reid, who would be the next territorial governor. Three others would represent the state in the United States Senate. Two would become governors after statehood was attained, five would serve on the state supreme court and five in the secession convention less than 25 years later. More than a third at the convention had previous legislative experience in other states.

The convention divided itself into 18 committees and all worked extremely hard to produce the final document which was adopted by a vote of 55-1 on January 4, 1839.

END OF THE WAR

After the capture of Osceola, the Second Seminole War became a series of small battles, repeated meetings which attempted to bargain for an end to the fighting and captures of small bands which were then shipped off to Indian Territory in Oklahoma.

Despite the hit-and-run turn the war took, it continued to cost hundreds of lives and the United States found itself unable to find a leader capable of bringing the war to a victorious end.

Officer after officer was shipped to Florida, took command, announced he had brought an end to the fighting and then departed in disgrace as a new battle flared someplace else in the territory.

However, the Indians were driven farther and farther south until most were concentrated in the area of the Everglades, deep in swamp country, where it was impossible for soldiers to follow and capture them.

Finally, in May 1841, Col. William Jenkins Worth was appointed commander of the U.S. troops in Florida. He decided to do what no other officer before him had done — to fight the Indians through the summer, despite the heat and insects.

Worth launched his summer campaign against Indian settlements and the crops they had planted on hammocks deep in the Everglade swamps. He destroyed their temporary towns and their food.

That proved to be more than the Indians could withstand and Chief Wild Cat, who had escaped from prison, led the last major defense before finally agreeing to surrender.

On February 14, 1842, Worth wrote to Gen. Winfield Scott, Commanding General of the Army, that the Indians were now so reduced in ability to fight back that hostilities could be said to be over.

By May, President John Tyler sent a special message to Congress, telling its members only about 240

Indians remained at large in Florida and that he was going to declare an end to the war.

He sent a message to Colonel Worth who then declared the war officially over on Aug. 14, 1842.

On a map, southern Florida doesn't look too different from northern Florida. But at the time the Seminoles were driven into southern Florida, it was a hot, swampy area much different from the pine forests of northern Florida.

Florida Enters the Union

The Seminole War had held back settlement in some parts of Florida but it was not enough to keep settlers out of all the territory.

In August 1842, just before the war ended officially, Congress passed a bill which made more than 200,000 acres of the territory available to new settlers. Any head of a family or a single man, more than 18 years old, could earn title to 160 acres of land by building a livable home and cultivating at least five acres of that land and living on it for five years.

In less than a year, nearly all of that 200,000 acres had been claimed.

The increase in population was great enough to make Florida eligible for statehood.

On March 3, 1845, Florida was admitted to the United States as the 27th state of the union.

The act meant the state now had complete home rule in local affairs and full participation in national government. Citizens could now choose their own state officials and manage and finance their own government. In Washington, they would be represented by two senators, appointed by the state legislature, and a representative, voted into that office by the people at large. While a territory, representation in Washington was limited to a non-voting delegate to the House of Representatives.

FIRST ELECTION

The first state election was scheduled for May 26, 1845.

The Democrats nominated William Dunn Moseley, a Jefferson County planter, to run for governor. The Whigs nominated Richard Keith Call, who had been territorial governor when the constitution was written.

Moseley defeated Call by 3,392 to 2,679 votes.

David Levy, also a Democrat, defeated Maj. Benjamin A. Putnam as Florida's first elected official in the U.S. House of Representatives.

On July 1, 1845, the state legislature elected James D. Westcott Jr. and David Levy to the United States Senate, thus creating an opening in the House. A new election had to be called to select a replacement for Levy.

Edward Cabell was elected in a close race but the loser, William Brockenbaugh contested the election and unseated Cabell. The fight over the seat went on until the election of 1846 when Cabell finally won.

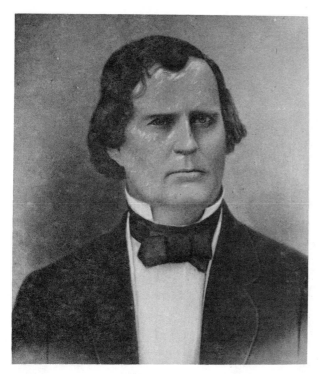

Madison Perry did not fear secession as did some other state officials. He called for immediate action to be taken if southern rights were threatened by Federal government.

Edward Carrington Cabel served two sessions in Congress.

THE ROAD TO SECESSION

In 1849, Thomas Brown was elected Florida's second governor; in 1853, James Broome became the third and, in 1857, Madison Starke Perry became the fourth man to hold that office.

During these years, tensions between the North and South increased. Florida, although a new state, quickly fell into line as a member of the Solid South.

That feeling was probably best represented by Gov. Perry, a staunch southerner.

Perry had been born in South Carolina in 1814 and came to Florida before statehood had been attained. He became a planter in Alachua County and represented that county in both the state house and senate. He was a member of the U.S. Senate in 1850 when the Compromise of 1850 was reached.

Under his administration as governor, railroads were given much encouragement and many new lines were opened in various parts of the state.

But, despite accomplishments of this type, Perry was an unswerving southerner. As early as 1858, predicting the possibility of secession, he urged re-establishment of the state militia. After Lincoln's nomination in the summer of 1860, Perry told state legislators that if Lincoln was elected, secession was certain to follow.

The state generally adopted that same attitude as the election of 1860 neared.

Summary: Florida, the State

Purchase of Florida by the United States in 1821 opened a new frontier for adventurous Americans along the eastern seaboard. Now it was no longer necessary for them to travel west to obtain new land. Gov. William Duval — who was to serve 12 years as territorial governor — quickly realized this area would grow. One of his first major moves was to find and establish a new capital site and, in 1824, Tallahassee was selected for that purpose. But, the influx of new settlers had other effects, as well. One of the things it caused was troubles with the Indians who were being crowded out of their traditional lands. As a result, in 1835, the Second Seminole War broke out in Florida. It lasted seven years before fighting ended. While the war was going on, a group of delegates met in St. Joseph and drew up a constitution against the day when Florida would achieve statehood. That day finally came in 1845 and Florida became the 27th member of the United States. However, as she joined the Union, pressures between North and South were growing to a peak. Florida would be faced, within 15 years, with a decision whether to remain a part of the United States or secede with other southern states.

Work Section

TRUE-FALSE

Answer the following questions true or false.

1. Tallahassee was selected as the territorial capital of Florida in 1824.
2. The territorial governor of Florida was elected.
3. The Treaty of Moultrie Creek set aside an area of Florida for an Indian reservation.
4. Gen. Wiley Thompson was an Indian agent.
5. Osceola was a chief of the Seminole tribe.
6. The first constitution was written in St. Joseph.
7. Col. William Worth commanded the Army in Florida when the Second Seminole War ended.
8. Florida was admitted to the United States as a state in 1832.

MULTIPLE CHOICE

Only one of the following answers is correct. Select the right one.

1. While Florida was a territory, it was represented in Washington by
   a. An elected representative
   b. A governor
   c. A senator
   d. None of the above

2. The Treaty of Payne's Landing called for the Indians to
   a. Move onto their reservation
   b. Quit fighting the Second Seminole War
   c. Agree to removal to Indian Territory
   d. Surrender all their guns

3. In the Dade Massacre, the Army lost
   a. 500 men
   b. 300 men
   c. 200 men
   d. None of the above

4. Osceola was captured
   a. While encamped near Tallahassee
   b. Under a flag of truce
   c. By Richard Keith Call
   d. By Gen. Jackson

5. Robert Raymond Reid was
   a. The first governor of Florida
   b. Chairman of the Constitutional Convention
   c. A United States Senator
   d. A general in the United States Army

6. The first elected governor of Florida as a state was
   a. Robert Raymond Reid
   b. Richard Keith Call
   c. William Duval
   d. William Moseley

7. The first man to represent Florida in the U.S. Senate was
   a. David Levy
   b. Benjamin Putnam
   c. William Moseley
   d. Thomas Brown

8. The two men who chose Tallahasseee as the site for the capital of Florida were John Lee Williams and
   a. Robert Raymond Reid
   b. David Levy
   c. Dr. William H. Simmons
   d. Gen. Andrew Jackson

COMPLETION

Fill in the blanks in the following sentences with the correct word or phrase.

1. _____ proclaimed Tallahassee the capital of Florida.
2. Indian Territory was what we now call _____
3. Ft. King was located where the present city of _____ stands.
4. Osceola died in captivity in _____
5. The first Florida constitution was adopted by a vote of _____
6. The Indian Coacoochee was known by white men as _____
7. The Second Seminole War ended in the year _____
8. Madison Starke Perry was _____ of Florida at the time of Abraham Lincoln's nomination.

SUGGESTED WORK PROJECTS

1. Using a map of Florida, locate the following places and tell why they were important.
   a. Tallahassee
   b. Moultrie Creek
   c. Bushnell
   d. Ocala
   e. Tampa
2. If possible, take your class on a field trip to the museum which now marks the site of the Dade Massacre.
3. If possible, take your class on a field trip to Constitutional Convention museum in Port St. Joe.

Part VI

Florida Leaves the Union
... and Returns

THE STATE IN 1860

What was Florida like as the election of 1860 neared?

First, she was still very much a frontier state. Her total population was about 140,000, only about half the number of people presently living in the city of St. Petersburg.

Of that number, almost half were slaves.

The main areas of population still centered around Pensacola in the west and St. Augustine in the east. The fastest growing section was between these two cities where cotton plantations were springing up at a rapid pace.

KING COTTON

At that time, cotton ranked as the only important crop in Florida, just as it ranked as the only important crop throughout the South.

Plantations were mostly large spreads of land. Because machinery was expensive and hard to come by, slaves toiled in the fields, planting, cultivating and picking the cotton crops.

Because the crop took so much out of the land, it became necessary for plantation owners to constantly buy additional land on which to grow cotton. This provided the main reason for the constant growth of individual plantations.

PLANTER POWER

But, because the South relied on such a single crop for its wealth, it also relied largely on planters for political influence. Although their number was small, their wealth was huge. And, much of that wealth was measured in the number of slaves they owned.

For this reason, the dispute over slavery played a large part in the election of 1860. The results of that election were at least a partial cause of southern states leaving the Union.

THE ELECTION OF 1860

Four men were nominated for the presidency. The Republicans chose Abraham Lincoln. The Democrats, unable to agree on one man, nominated Stephen Douglas and John Brackenridge and John Bell's name was put into the race by the Constitutional Union party.

Lincoln, as we know, was elected when he got 180 electoral votes. Combined, the other candidates had more popular votes, but divided the remaining 123 electoral votes between them. Not a single vote was cast for Lincoln in the entire state of Florida.

Secession and War Begin

Lincoln's election became the signal for disappointed southerners to choose to leave the Union. South Carolina was first, making its decision in December, 1860, and opening the way for other southern states to follow.

The Florida convention to decide whether to follow South Carolina was held in Tallahasseee in January, 1861. On January 10, it voted 62-7 to leave the United States after it had been a state for only 15 years.

On February 4, 1861, Florida's representatives joined those from five other southern states at a convention in Montgomery, Alabama. They met to draw up a

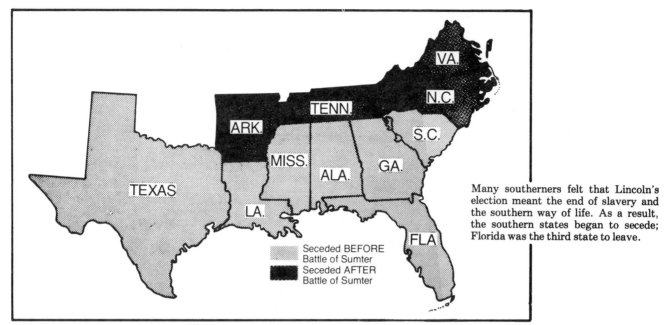

Many southerners felt that Lincoln's election meant the end of slavery and the southern way of life. As a result, the southern states began to secede; Florida was the third state to leave.

constitution for a new nation, the Confederate States of America. Five days later, they elected Jefferson Davis president of the new country.

THE WAR BEGINS

Warlike preparations had begun throughout the South long before secession was voted and Florida was no different than the other states.

As early as November 1860, just a few days after Lincoln had been elected, 83 men in Madison formed a company willing to fight for the South.

Days before Florida voted to secede, efforts were made to seize Federal arsenals in some parts of the state to assure they would not be destroyed when secession took place. As early as Jan. 5, 1861, the Quincy Guards took over the arsenal at Chattahoochee.

Within days after secession, other efforts were made in such cities as Pensacola and Key West to cap-

An old photo of a Confederate gun battery, 1861.

ture Federal installations in those cities. Most of these efforts were unsuccessful.

But, when actual fighting began, the battles in Florida were very limited.

There was reason for this.

First, Florida was far from land armies of the North. Second, most Federal action in Florida was conducted by Navy units. There were very few face-to-face meetings between United States Navy troops and Florida Army troops. Third, most Florida volunteers were sent north where their actions could be directed against Northern armies.

FIGHTING IN FLORIDA

However, there were some isolated battles and some instances of unusual meetings between Confederate and Union forces. And, such actions as there were produced some heroes who are still revered in the state.

One of the earliest incidents occurred in Tampa Bay.

Tampa Bay was blockaded by Federal ships almost from the very beginning of the war. Despite that, blockade runners continued to operate in the area.

One of the most successful blockade-runners was Tampa's Captain James McKay. When Federal blockaders, stationed at Egmont Key, got word of his activities, they decided to stop him.

On Oct. 17, 1862, two Federal gunboats moved into Tampa Bay and began shelling Ft. Brooke and the city. Most of the people fled into the nearby woods. After dark, 85 Yankees landed near what is now known as Gadsden Point.

This group marched up the Hillsborough River. Six

miles above the city they located two of McKay's ships. Both were set afire and destroyed. The Federals then started back down the river.

Near what is now known as Ballast Point, the group was attacked by some of the Tampa militiamen who had returned when the shelling stopped.

In the fight, three Union men were killed, twelve wounded and three taken prisoner. The Tampa group lost six men killed, had several wounded and lost seven prisoners to the Yankees.

THE BIGGEST BATTLE

Perhaps the best known land battle in Florida was the Battle of Olustee, often called the only major battle fought in Florida during the Civil War.

The battle took place in 1864 when Union transports brought troops up the St. Johns River to Jacksonville. Within three days, those troops had marched more than 30 miles westward into Florida.

As the Union soldiers advanced, General Joseph Finegan, Commander of the District of East Florida, retreated, awaiting reinforcements. Finally, he elected to make a stand. He selected a site at Olustee, 13 miles east of Lake City.

Fighting began on February 20, 1864, about noon. The battle lasted only about six hours but Federal losses were so high, Northern troops were forced to retreat and the threat was over. The South lost 93 killed and had 847 wounded. The North lost 203 killed, had 1,152 wounded and 506 missing in action.

In addition, the South captured five cannons, 1,600 rifles and handguns and 130,000 rounds of ammunition. All this equipment was badly needed.

Most history books call the Battle of Olustee a Southern victory.

GENERAL FINEGAN

Finegan became commander of East Florida in April 1862, when Floridians protested the defensive policies of Confederate forces in the state, then under command of Brig. Gen. James H. Trapier. The protested policy called for Confederate troops to be held in readiness in the state's interior and to move into fighting position only if an area along the coast was threatened by invasion.

The change in command did not change the policy but Finegan was more diplomatic than Trapier. He was even able to prevail upon private citizens to give up their weapons so he could equip a regiment which had none of its own. Among the items he obtained were shotguns, rifles and muskets.

General Joseph Finegan's first wartime orders were to defend the Apalachicola and St. John's rivers.

CAPTAIN DICKISON

While Gen. Finegan was called upon to fight only the Battle of Olustee, Capt. John J. Dickison, a Florida cavalryman, was active throughout the war and fought one of the strangest battles of that war.

Just three months after the Battle of Olustee, several Federal gunboats made their way up the St. Johns River, protecting a number of transports carrying soldiers who were seeking to capture Captain John J. Dickison, a Florida cavalryman who was raiding Federal outposts.

Dickison had a two-gun artillery company with him at the time and decided to attempt an ambush of some of the boats. He placed his artillery in a clump of trees near Palatka. When the gunboat COLUMBINE anchored for the night, he fired upon it and disabled the boat. As it floated downstream, his sharpshooters opened fire, killing many members of the crew. The boat finally grounded on a sandbar and was captured. All but 66 members of its crew died in the attack and many of the survivors were severely wounded.

The Palatka battle is the only case in the Civil War in which a ship was captured by a unit of the Army.

Dickison was a Virginian who came to Florida with his family in 1856 and settled near Ocala. Shortly after the war broke out, he helped form a volunteer unit known as the Marion Light Artillery.

It became one of the outstanding units in the state, fighting a number of small skirmishes, conducting raids and scouting expeditions and keeping Union forces in Florida constantly off-balance.

There is a story which claims that Federal Army personnel referred to the guerrilla leader Dickison as Dixie and the area in which he operated as Dixie's Land (Dixieland). Some romantic writers think that may have been where the term originated.

Dickison returned to his home near Ocala when the war was over. In 1899 he wrote "Military History of Florida" which is still considered one of the best reference books ever written about the state's Civil war period.

He died at his home in 1902 and was buried in Evergreen Cemetery in Jacksonville. The Ocala Banner paid tribute by calling him "the most conspicuous soldier Florida contributed to the Civil War."

John Dickison headed a group of soldiers known as the Irregulars, or soldiers not members of the regular Army forces.

UNCONQUERED CAPITAL

Although fighting was very limited in Florida, the state had the distinction of being the only Confederate state whose capital was not captured by Union forces. Early in 1865, the last year of the war, an effort was made to capture Tallahassee but came to disaster for the Union invaders.

The operation began March 3, 1865 when a party of approximately 30 Federal troops landed near the mouth of East River, surprised pickets at the Ocklocknee railroad bridge and captured that important span.

The following morning, several ships entered the channel and landed a number of supporting troops. They began a slow movement up river, toward Tallahassee.

By late that evening, word of the invasion reached

A union sentinel tower, 1864. Access to the tower was gained by a ladder in the center of the tower base. Such towers were used for message relay and lookout purposes.

the capital city and a call was issued for volunteers. A force of more than 600 was raised, among them several cadets from the West Florida Seminary, some barely 14 years old.

The two groups, Union invaders, and southern defenders, began moving toward each other on March 5, 1865 and met near the point where the St. Marks River goes underground, commonly called Natural Bridge.

There they met in a pitched battle which lasted until late in the afternoon. Union losses were heavy, estimated to have been more than 150 men, while the Rebels lost but three in their defense.

The Union troops were driven into retreat, marched back down river and boarded their boats.

Just a bit more than a month later, the war ended, with Tallahassee still unconquered.

These small battles were typical of the fighting in Florida.

CIVILIAN CONTRIBUTIONS

This is not to say that Florida did not make a contribution to the Confederate war effort. Florida's main contribution was the supplies it was able to contribute to the Southern cause.

All across the state, groups called the Ladies Military Aid Organization were formed. Their job was to make clothing for the soldiers going into service and to do whatever else was possible to help in the war effort.

The ladies had several sources of help. Several times, the Legislature voted to give them state money to help buy cloth to be made into uniforms. At other times, donations were asked from civilians to aid in paying for the help supplied. Sometimes the donations came in the form of money, sometimes in the form of foods, especially such items as oranges, limes and grapefruit.

Among the contributions the ladies made was the opening of a 150-bed hospital in Richmond, Virginia, to care for sick and wounded Florida men fighting in that area. In just the first year that it was open, it provided help for more than 1,000 patients.

Dr. Samuel Mudd unknowingly treated John Wilkes Booth, the killer of President Lincoln. Because Dr. Mudd had aided a criminal, he was sentenced to life imprisonment at Ft. Jefferson, in the Dry Tortugas. While he was there, he was called upon to treat the victims of a yellow fever epidemic. Was the decision to punish Dr. Mudd fair? Why or why not?

FOOD PRODUCTS

The state's main contribution to the South was food. Warehouses were set up at several cities within the state where meat, vegetables, fruits, grains, sugar and salt were collected to be sent to armies fighting in other parts of the country.

Mistresses of plantations, men too old to bear arms and youngsters too young to fight worked and managed· the farms. They were aided, in most cases, by blacks.

President Lincoln had issued his Emancipation Proclamation at the beginning of the war, on Jan. 1, 1863, but most blacks chose to remain on the plantations and farms they had called home all their lives.

Because money was very scarce in Florida, many of these items were often taken from farmers with a promise to pay at a later date. When the South lost the war, these promises were not always kept. This caused some dissatisfaction among farmers and, as the end of the war began to draw nearer, it produced many cases of hoarding and outlaw trading, commonly called blackmarketing.

Maybe the two largest items Florida supplied to the southern war effort were beef cattle and salt.

Cattle growing had become the second-largest farming effort in Florida, with only cotton more important. Unlike cotton, whose market was very limited in the South, cattle were always in demand. More important, they could be driven on foot to points where they could be used to feed the armies. Florida cattle growers became the main source of supply to southern armies fighting in Georgia and South Carolina.

SALT MAKING

Salt was one of those items which was very important but which was largely imported before the war. It was important because most fresh meats were preserved by its use; refrigeration did not exist and ice was in very short supply.

Most of the salt in Florida was made by putting sea water through a boiling process or through use of salt beds.

In the first method, salt water was placed in huge kettles and boiled away. The salt was left and packaged for later use. This process was used at Cedar Key but the plant there was destroyed when a raiding party came ashore and wrecked the equipment.

Salt beds were large, shallow holes dug into the ground. Sea water was allowed to flow into them. The sun then evaporated the water, leaving the salt to be gathered.

Although both processes were rather slow, salt sold for as much as $1 a pound. As a result, many people went into the salt-making business and many plants were opened along the state's sea coasts.

Such methods were discontinued when huge salt deposits were found in the west and cheaper and more efficient means of extracting salt became a business. Salt could then be purchased more cheaply from stores than it could be produced by these outdated methods.

A salt factory on Florida's gulf coast, just before the factory's destruction by the Union forces shown in the picture.

As the War Ended

THE 13TH AMENDMENT

The end of the war meant changes throughout the South and Florida was no exception to that rule. For example, on Dec. 18, 1865, the 13th Amendment to the Constitution was declared ratified.

It proclaimed:

"Neither slavery nor involuntary servitude, except as a punishment for crime whereof the party shall have been duly convicted, shall exist within the United States, or any place subject to their jurisdiction."

To the slave, it meant he was free to work for himself. It also meant that he would meet with much resistance and sometimes hatred from former owners and poorer whites with whom he would now compete for jobs.

BLACK CODES

To counter these new rights, many Southern states (Florida included) adopted special rules called Black Codes. These were laws passed to be specially applied to the newly freed blacks. Some examples included:

Blacks were authorized to testify in legal cases involving their own race but could not give evidence against whites.

Special penalties, such as whipping, were ordered rather than imprisonment.

Death sentences were decreed for rape of a white woman by a black but no mention of punishment was made for similar assaults by white men on black women.

Intermarriage between races was forbidden.

Segregation was approved for public meetings and on public transportation.

THE 14TH AMENDMENT

On June 13, 1866, the United States Congress proposed the 14th Amendment to the Constitution. This amendment was a sweeping, four-part clause which further complicated the right of Southern states to return to membership in the United States.

It was ratified on July 28, 1868 but, earlier in the year, Florida had adopted a new state constitution which included many of the required items and was considered acceptable enough to allow Florida to return to the Union. Military rule in the state ended and Florida again was declared a state on July 4, 1868.

OUTSTANDING BLACKS

One of the clauses of the state constitution granted blacks the right to vote. As a result, in the new elections, several blacks won office and several others were appointed to high positions.

Among the most outstanding of these were such men as Josiah Walls, who was elected to the United States Congress, and Jonathan Gibbs, who served as secretary of State and Superintendent of Public Instruction.

JONATHAN GIBBS

Gibbs was born in Philadelphia in 1827, the son of a Methodist minister. His father died while Jonathan was very young and he was forced to go to work as a carpenter. However, he stayed close to religion and became a minister in the Presbyterian Church at a very young age. Members of that church were so impressed with his ability, they sent him to school at Dartmouth College where he won a degree. Later he took additional work at Princeton.

His church decided to send him to Florida to work with newly-freed blacks when the war ended. In Florida he came to the attention of Harrison Reed. When Reed was elected governor in 1868, he appointed Gibbs his Secretary of State.

Jonathan Gibbs set about improving Florida's educational system.

Gibbs served in that position for more than four years and won the respect of almost everyone in the state. When Reed was defeated for re-election by Governor Ossian B. Hart, Hart appointed Gibbs State Superintendent of Public Instruction, the highest educational post in the state.

When he became director, more than 71,000 of the state's 200,000 population was considered illiterate — meaning they could neither read nor write. Most were blacks who had spent their lives on plantations. Gibbs set about correcting this. He improved the school system and in just about a year managed to triple enrollment.

What was more important, he managed to provide schools for blacks and increase the number of them attending to the point where almost a third of all students in the state were blacks.

He adopted standard textbooks and standard courses of study for the first time in the state's history. Much of the state's modern school system still is based on the work he did. Gibbs died in 1874 while still in office. Gibbs High School in St. Petersburg is named for this man. No other black has ever served at the cabinet level in a state administration.

While Gibbs was appointed to the two major offices he held, Walls was elected by the voters of Florida.

JOSIAH WALLS

Like Gibbs, Walls was not a native Floridian. He was born of free parents in Winchester, Virginia in 1842 and became a miller by trade. When the war broke out, Walls became a servant to a Confederate officer. He was captured during the battle of Yorktown in May 1862 and joined the Union Army.

After fighting in several battles and being promoted to sergeant, he was sent to Jacksonville as an instructor. When the war ended, he decided to stay in Florida and settled near Alachua.

In 1867, he went to Tallahassee as a delegate to the state Republican Convention. The following year he was elected to the state House of Representatives. In 1869, he was elected to the state Senate. The following summer he was nominated to run for United States congressman.

He won the election from Silas L. Niblack and went to Washington. While he was there Niblack contested the election and had it overturned. In spite of everything Niblack could do, Walls was re-elected in 1872 and again in 1874 before finally being defeated in 1876.

During these years, he was Florida's only congressman in the House of Representatives in Washington and he made a number of very important contributions to improvements in the state. Among those were the grant of 90,000 acres of land to the trustees of the Florida Agricultural College.

Many customs houses, post offices and other federal buildings were built in the state during the time he was in office and mail service was greatly improved.

When he left politics, he returned to farming and was in charge of the farm at the State College at Tallahassee when he died in 1905.

Josiah Walls, shown here in an old photograph, was elected to three successive terms as a United States Congressman.

POLITICAL CHANGES

It is important to note that both Gibbs and Walls were members of the Republican party. There was a reason for this. In the national government, it was the Republican party which was responsible for most legislation meant to give blacks more equal rights. As a result, when they obtained the right to vote, they became members of that party.

On the other hand, most whites were intent on keeping the black "in his place" and remained members of the Democratic party.

The Republican party was further strengthened by northerners who came South to aid the blacks in their fight for equality. These people were known as carpetbaggers. The combination of carpetbaggers and blacks gave the Republicans a majority which lasted for several years and is generally referred to as the Reconstruction Period.

OTHER CHANGES

Many other changes were also brought about after the war. For example, cotton production, the largest industry in Florida before the Civil War, dropped off sharply and never recovered its importance.

On the other hand, farm products and livestock production began to increase. Most of the new farms were much smaller than the cotton plantations before the war.

The reason for the agricultural change was that freed blacks no longer were bound to plantations, many obtaining small plots of land to farm for themselves.

Other changes which helped to change life in Florida included the desire for more and cheaper land. That caused many men, both white and black, to begin pushing into the unsettled middle of the state and to areas further south.

The St. Johns and Halifax Railroad, 1866. This was one of the first passenger trains operating after the Civil War.

Railroad development, which was very limited before the Civil War, helped these pioneers in their efforts to reach fertile, unclaimed lands.

Schools began to change as the blacks were allowed to join the public school system — although still on the basis of what the South called "separate but equal schools."

New industries began growing in the state. The lumber industry for example, became one of the biggest.

Summary: How the War Changed Florida

In short, the Florida which had left the Union and joined the Confederacy to fight the Civil War, was never to return in its original form.

The struggle between black and white had only begun in the years following the war. However, there was little question but what doors were beginning to open through which blacks could seek success. It was also evident that the plantation-oriented Southern aristocracy, while not yet dead, was beginning to lose its influence.

Other states were more affected than Florida by the fighting in the Civil War. Because of the limited number of battles in Florida, war damage was not as great.

However, in the Reconstruction years which followed, Florida did undergo changes very much the same as those elsewhere in the South.

Political parties became sharply divided on policies, especially in the areas of black-white relations.

The state also began a period of growth far exceeding what had gone before. Unlike most other Southern states, Florida still had a great deal of unsettled land. Its mild climate and the cheapness of that land attracted many pioneers, much as the situation was in the West.

In many ways, because of the newcomers, Florida's development after the Civil War followed more closely along the lines of western development than Southern.

Work Section

TRUE-FALSE

Answer the following questions true or false.

1. In the Presidential election of 1860, Abraham Lincoln got more votes in Florida than anyone else.
2. The convention which met to decide whether the state should leave the United States voted 62-7 in favor of the move.
3. Florida played a large role in the actual fighting during the Civil War.
4. The site of the largest battle in the state was Olustee.
5. The making of salt was a major business in the state during the Civil War.
6. Cattle farming became the second largest farming effort in Florida during the Civil War.
7. Florida's cotton growing industry was not upset as a result of the Civil War.
8. Florida was one of the few Southern states which did not have Union military rule in the years after the war ended.
9. Jonathan Gibbs was the first black ever to serve in the state cabinet.

MULTIPLE CHOICE

Only one of the following answers is correct. Make the right one.

1. Before the Civil War, Florida's largest industry was
   a. Cotton growing
   b. Fishing
   c. Making salt
   d. None of the above
2. Florida voted to leave the United States in
   a. November 1862
   b. March 1863
   c. January 1861
   d. December 1862
3. The first volunteer company in Florida was formed
   a. Before the vote to leave the United States
   b. After the vote to leave the United States
4. Captain John J. Dickison won fame as
   a. A leading cotton plantation owner
   b. An outstanding Southern naval hero
   c. Governor of the state
   d. None of the above
5. The Ladies Military Aid Organization was
   a. A group of women soldiers
   b. Ladies who made clothing for Florida's soldiers
   c. A group of nurses
   d. None of the above
6. Union ships prevented Confederate ships from leaving Florida ports during the war and this was called
   a. Raiding the port
   b. Blockading
   c. Target practice
   d. Maneuvers
7. Special laws were written to control freed slaves and they were called
   a. Amendments
   b. The Constitution
   c. Black Codes
   d. None of the above
8. The Reconstruction period was
   a. The last year of the Civil War
   b. The election of William Marvin as governor
   c. The law which allowed blacks to vote
   d. A period of several years after the war ended

9. Dr. Samuel Mudd treated yellow fever at
   a. Fort Jefferson
   b. All over the state during the war
   c. A settlement near Tampa Bay
   d. None of the above

COMPLETION

Fill in the blank in the following sentences with the correct word or phrase.

1. In 1860, Florida had a population of _____ people.
2. The convention of Southern states which met to form the Confederate States of America was held in
3. The only battle during the Civil War in which a ship was captured by land forces was the Battle of
4. _____ was considered one of the most successful blockade-runners in Florida during the Civil War.
5. One of the major salt producing cities in Florida during the war was
6. Florida's greatest contribution to the war effort was
7. The 13th Amendment to the Constitution made it
8. The Reconstruction period is generally said to have ended when

9. Josiah Walls was the first black elected from the state to serve in the _____ in Washington.

SUGGESTED WORK PROJECTS

A. Using a map of Florida, locate the following places and tell why they were important.
   1. Olustee
   2. Palatka
   3. Tampa Bay
   4. Cedar Key
   5. Tallahassee
   6. Ocala
   7. Ft. Jefferson
   8. Bradenton
   9. St. Augustine
   10. Pensacola

B. Using a small, shallow pan, make salt by the evaporation method of setting salt water in the sun.
C. Contact the local historical society and ask a member of that organization to take students through the local historical museum.
D. Plan field trip visits to nearby cities where Civil War events occurred.
   1. Gamble Mansion, Bradenton
   2. Historical marker for Ft. Brooke, downtown Tampa
   3. Yulee Sugar Mill, Homosassa Springs

Part VII
A Period of Growth: Tourism Begins

RETURN OF THE DEMOCRATS

In 1877 George Franklin Drew took office as the 12th governor of the state of Florida. He was a Democrat, the first to be elected to that office since the end of the Civil War.

His election marked the beginning of a long period of Democratic rule, a period which helped to bring the term "one-party system" to the south.

However, because the Republicans were unable to regain control of the state, it did not mean a period of political peace.

Whites of almost every walk of life joined the Democratic Party because it was known as the white man's party. They were determined to keep blacks from political power. However, because most party members had so many different political aims, unrest was nearly as great as it might have been with two or more separate parties.

During Reconstruction days, most of the public lands in Florida had been reserved for homesteaders. But, one of the restrictions for those seeking to settle on these lands was that they had to have been loyal to the United States during the Civil War. Because so many pre-Civil War residents in Florida had fought for the Confederacy, they were not eligible.

That meant that most homestead lands were opened only to two classes of people. These were the freedmen — blacks who had been slaves but were made free by the Emancipation Proclamation — and people who would migrate to Florida from Northern states.

When the Democrats regained control of the state after the 1877 election, they were able to change the laws and open the sale of unclaimed lands to anyone who wished to buy them.

Growth of the Railroads

At the same time, special favors were being shown to railroads.

Many thousands of acres of these homestead lands were turned into farms as newcomers settled on them. However, most of these farms were in very isolated areas which were not reached by roads. In order for farmers to get their crops to market, it became necessary to build railroads which could carry their products.

Building railroads was a very expensive undertaking. Therefore, the state gave thousands of acres of land to railroad builders, along which they would be able to lay their rails. In that manner, they could connect outlying farms with market places.

That put the railroads into the land business, as well. Because farms were so few and far between, it was not always profitable for railroads because the amount of produce being moved was limited. So, they began bringing new settlers of their own into these areas, selling them land along the right-of-way at reduced prices. This meant more farms and therefore more business for the railroad.

Floating lumber down the Oklawaha River. The lumber industry grew along with homesteading and railroad building.

Thus, the development of railroads worked in two ways. It made it easier for farmers already on the land to get their crops to market. And, it also made more land available to farmers, attracting many hundreds of newcomers to the state.

Therefore, as railroads grew, so did Florida's population.

There were also drawbacks to this system.

Railroads, because they were the fastest and often the only means of transporting crops between farm and market, charged almost anything they wished. This method became known as "anything the traffic will bear."

And, because the railroads took this attitude, many farmers began demanding that railroad owners be regulated in order to protect the farmer from impossible freight prices.

THE POPULIST REVOLT

By the 1880s, farmers had decided they would have to organize to protect themselves. They gathered enough political power to elect state government officials who then helped them get a fair deal from the railroads.

This became known as the Populist Revolt.

During state elections of the 1880s, many candidates who campaigned on a platform of railroad regulation were elected, most of them because of solid support from the farmers. The first to actually do something to help the farmers, however, was Gov. Edward A. Perry, who was elected in 1884.

In 1887, he recommended a railroad commission be established in the state and the Legislature passed such a law. The law created a three-man commission which was authorized to establish passenger and freight rates, set regulations and require railroads to adopt uniform classifications for freight of all kinds.

Picking cotton on a Florida plantation, late 1890's. Even the littlest children had to help. Were there any Child Labor Laws at that time?

Waiting for cotton to be ginned. Look closely at the upper left corner and you'll see two more men, covered with cotton.

In other words, the commission had the power to tell the railroads, "You can only charge this much to move a bushel of corn. You cannot charge so much to move corn from this area and another price for another area."

Unfortunately, the railroads had gained so much power in the years of their growth, many refused to comply with these regulations and the commission was unable to force them to obey.

THE FLORIDA GRANGE

The commission's failure set off a new round of fighting and led to even more organization by the farmers.

In 1867, similar conditions in the Midwest had driven farmers there to found an organization called the National Grange of the Patrons of Husbandry. It became known simply as the Grange. The aim at the time of its organization was to bring farmers together in social and educational organizations. Basically, it was not a political organization.

Six years later, in 1873, the first Grange chapter was formed in Florida and soon the organization was enjoying rapid growth in this state.

While it was not political, it did provide a means for meetings of farmers who could discuss common problems and railroads were one of the largest of these problems. Out of the Grange, as a result of these meetings, came another organization, this one called the Farmers Alliance. This organization did become very political.

By 1890, the new group was so strong it had been responsible for the election of a number of members of the Florida Legislature. It now began making demands on those members for new laws establishing railroad controls and, this time, laws which could be enforced.

The national convention of the Alliance met in Ocala in 1890 and issued a list of demands called the Ocala Demands. Many of these were for railroad regulation.

Also on the list were demands for the abolition of national banks, a graduated income tax, free and unlimited coinage of silver, two per cent loans for farmers on perishable products and election of U.S. Senators by direct vote of the people.

Unfortunately, the demands were too many and too strong. The Legislature refused to pass most of them.

FURTHER GROWTH OF RAILROADS

The continued lack of regulation left railroad owners in a position of unlimited expansion. This had both good and bad results.

The good was contained in a boom of new building, bringing rail transportation to parts of the state which never had seen trains before.

The bad, on the other hand, helped contribute to a financial panic in 1893 and the depression which followed. Many farmers and citrus growers throughout the state went broke and a number of smaller railroads were bankrupted by the crash.

Railroad Tycoons

The condition of railroads in Florida brought two powerful men onto the scene. They soon became two of the most powerful in the state's history.

They were Henry Bradley Plant and Henry Morrison Flagler.

Between them, they created the Seaboard Coast Line Railroad and the Florida East Coast Railway, the two largest railroads in the state.

HENRY PLANT

Plant was born in Connecticut in 1819, the son of farming parents, and spent a very undistinguished youth.

When the Civil War broke out in 1861, Plant was living in Augusta, Ga., representing a New York firm in that area.

Confederate States President Jefferson Davis chose him to be in charge of express shipments for the new country. His responsibilities included Army pay and special dispatches between fighting units.

By the time the war ended, his reputation was great enough that he was able to bridge the gap between Northern businessmen, who wanted to invest huge sums of money they had made during the war, and Southern developers, who were anxious to help in putting their section of the country back on its feet.

With the aid of Col. Henry S. Ames, the man who had been railroad chief for Gen. Robert E. Lee during the war, Plant began investing many of the Northern dollars available to him in some of the Southern railroads which were in financial trouble.

When the state began offering land bonuses to railroads for each mile of track they laid, Plant decided to get into the railroad business as deeply as possible. Enlisting some New York millionaires, he formed the Plant Investment Co. and began buying up some of the smaller railroads which had money problems.

By 1883, he had railroad tracks across much of the state and thousands of acres of land under his control.

Tampa became his headquarters and, at that city, he added a steamship line to his vast holdings. In 1888, he entered yet another business, building the Tampa Bay Hotel, one of the largest of its kind in the world.

The Tampa Bay Hotel became headquarters for officers during the Spanish-American War. Before this, the hotel had been one of the grandest in all Florida.

HENRY FLAGLER

Flagler was a johnny-come-lately in Florida in comparison to Plant but he was a much wealthier man when he did become interested in the state.

He entered the business world at a very young age, became a success during the Civil War and then went broke when that war ended.

At age 36, he met John D. Rockefeller and, two years after he had gone broke, became a partner in Rockefeller, Andrews and Flagler. The firm became the base on which Standard Oil was built. By 1890, 23 years after the partnership was formed, the Standard Oil Trust was the biggest monopoly the world had ever seen.

Flagler's first visit to Florida came in 1878 when he brought his wife to Jacksonville for her health. Six years later, after his first wife had died and he had remarried, he brought his new wife to Florida on their honeymoon. This time, he chose the city of St. Augustine for his trip.

There was only one drawback about reaching St. Augustine. The railroad line ran only as far as Jacksonville. There, the multi-millionaire had to leave his private railroad car and continue on to St. Augustine by boat.

When he returned the following year, he decided to build a massive hotel for northern visitors such as himself. In order to make it easier for these visitors to get to it, he bought a small railroad, built some bridges and ran the line all the way to St. Augustine. His hotel was called the Ponce de Leon.

That first small line was the start of Flagler's railroad empire. In succeeding years, he pushed this basic line farther and farther south along the east coast of the state, built several more hotels, bought up a number of smaller railroads and combined them into a system which he renamed the Florida East Coast Railway.

Florida and the Spanish-American War

The rapid growth of railroads throughout the state came none too soon for the good of the country.

On February 15, 1898, the U.S. battleship Maine blew up in Havana harbor with the loss of 260 American lives.

The outcry which followed swept the country into war with Spain and, because Florida was the closest point in the United States to Cuba, it became a center of preparations for that war.

Soldiers from all over the United States were sent to Florida by rail where they were trained before moving on to Cuba to invade that island country and help it to gain its independence from Spain.

Literally thousands of young men began making campsites in Tampa and Jacksonville. Tampa harbor was filled with ships which were to move them on to the invasion.

The Navy concentrated the majority of its efforts in Key West and soon newspaper men from all over the world were flooding into all three of these cities.

The Tampa Bay Hotel, built by Henry Plant in 1888, just 10 years earlier, became the headquarters for some of the most colorful military and journalistic figures this country has ever known.

Col. Theodore Roosevelt, who would be elected President of the United States just three years later,

Training for the Spanish-American War. The soldiers would hide behind their horses during gun battles. This sort of battle was hard on the horses.

Busing in 1898. Buses like this wagonette were used in Duval county to transport children to school.

brought his famous Rough Riders into Tampa.

And, Winston Churchill, who would be prime minister of England during World War II, spent some time in Tampa, as well, writing dispatches for British papers about the Spanish-American War.

The first American troops dispatched to Cuba left Tampa at 3:30 on the morning of June 14, 1898. Thirty-five transport ships, carrying more than 16,000 men, moved out of the harbor under cover of darkness. Two months later, the first transports left Fernandina, taking most of the men from camps around Jacksonville.

For several months, men streamed into and out of both these major staging areas. The railroads, built by Plant and Flagler, played a major role in moving both the men and their equipment.

The harbor at Key West was equally busy, moving freight and animals to the fighting in Cuba and serving as a main base for naval operations.

The war lasted only until August 12, 1899 but it was a busy time for Florida and the United States and the railroads made millions of dollars as a result of the unexpected business.

GROWTH OF THE GOLD COAST

When peace returned, the expanded railroads found themselves with more equipment and more miles of rail than they had customers for. But, that was not the type of situation which would discourage such men as Plant and Flagler.

Flagler's lines, for instance, now reached as far south as Miami and he controlled more than two-million acres of land along those lines. Additionally, he had built a number of plush resort hotels which catered to the very wealthy winter visitors.

Flagler began selling off his land at $1.50 to $5 per acre, aiming primarily at new settlers who would farm the lands and provide produce which his railroads would then haul to market.

He also started a publicity campaign in northern cities which told of the sub-tropical beauty of Florida during the winter months and his hotels began filling up with rich businessmen who wanted to get away from the cold and snow of northern winters.

So popular did the lower east coast of the state become among these wealthy visitors, it soon became known as the Gold Coast. Moreover, many of the people who first came to stay in Flagler hotels, soon bought land and built their own huge, expensive homes, creating brand new cities such as Palm Beach.

The first Florida boom was under way.

Making cigars in Tampa, early 1900's. Eventually, the cigar factories would hire readers to read newspapers and books to the men as the men rolled cigars.

61

Napoleon Broward took a firm stand for the draining of the Everglades, humane treatment of convicts, and a better educational system. He was against the sale of liquor in Florida.

THE BROWARD ERA

The first boom brought many men to prominence in Florida history but, aside from the railroad barons we already have mentioned, probably none was more colorful than Napoleon Bonaparte Broward.

Broward was born on a farm in Duval County on April 19, 1857, became an orphan at the age of 12 and worked in a number of jobs just to keep his young body and soul together. He worked in a logging camp at the age of 14, then as a farmhand, a steamboat roustabout, cod fisherman on the Grand Banks of Newfoundland and a river boat pilot on the St. Johns River.

Just before the Spanish-American War broke out, he bought his own steam tug and christened it the Three Friends. Determined to help Cuba gain its independence from Spain, he made a total of eight trips between Jacksonville and Cuba with war supplies, running the Spanish blockade of the island to complete his missions.

After the war, he decided to go into politics and twice was elected sheriff of Duval County, a Jacksonville city councilman and a member of the state House of Representatives before deciding to run for governor.

He was elected governor in 1904 and served in that office until January 1909. His term was a stormy one in which he offered a number of bold programs, most of which were controversial.

Many succeeded and many failed. Among his successes was the consolidation of the state's higher educa-

tion system from seven into four schools. Other accomplishments included a child labor law, better salaries for state employees and the building of a governor's mansion.

In 1908, before his term as governor expired, he ran for the U.S. Senate and was defeated. He tried again and won in 1910. However, Broward never went to the Senate because he died before his term in Washington started.

Many of the ideas which Broward had worked so hard to enact into law during his administration were passed on and picked up by the two governors who followed him in office —Albert Gilchrist and Park Trammel. This 12-year period has come to be known as the Broward Era in honor of the man who started the changes.

A RAILROAD GOES TO SEA

In 1904, the Spanish-American War had been history for five years and Henry Flagler celebrated his 74th birthday. But, despite his age, his wealth and his accomplishments, he still was determined to write yet another chapter of railroad history.

That was the year he announced that he was going to extend his Florida East Coast Railway from Miami, 155 miles to Key West.

People had questioned his wisdom when he announced, years before, that he was going to build a railroad from Jacksonville to Miami. Now they were certain the old man had gone completely crazy.

They pointed out he would have to span more than 75 miles of open water and that had **never** been accomplished before in railroad history.

That didn't stop Flagler.

During the construction of the Key West Railroad, pictured above, Flagler observed "No one has any business being connected with this who cannot stand grief." What did he mean?

He knew Cuba's new independence would mean a great deal of added trade for the United States. He knew also that Havana was only 90 miles from Key West and that most of that Cuban trade would come through the latter city. Finally, he knew that when the Panama Canal, which had been started the same year, was completed, it would have to be protected by the U.S. Navy. That meant a huge naval base somewhere in the southern United States and Key West was the most logical place for it.

All of these factors added up to two-way traffic for his proposed rail line — coal to be hauled to Key West for the Navy and Cuban products to be brought back from there for sale elsewhere in the United States.

It took eight years to complete the project but complete it Flagler did. At times, there were as many as 30,000 men engaged in the job. At least 300 died in the task, several in one of the two hurricanes which delayed progress.

But, on Jan. 22, 1912, Flagler, now 82 years old, rode the first train from Miami to Key West and stepped off his car to a huge celebration in his honor.

Sixteen months later, he died at Whitehall, his famous $2.5 million home in Palm Beach, a city he had virtually created.

Summary: Development Begins

In the years that followed Reconstruction in Florida, the state enjoyed a period of almost unbelieveable growth. Railroads were as responsible for much of that growth as any other single factor. Farmers began settling along newly established lines and business boomed as their crops were transported to market. Then, Henry Bradley Plant and Henry Morrison Flagler came onto the scene. Between them, they bought up most of the small feeder lines and consolidated them into two large lines, the Florida East Coast Railway and the Seaboard Coast Line. Both added to the state's growth by promoting Florida as a winter resort for wealthy northerners. When the Spanish-American War broke out, Florida, because it was so close to Cuba, became a center for military preparation and the railroads profited even more. By the time the war ended, Florida's future had been decided. But, Flagler foresaw even more advancement and built his railroad from Miami to Key West, one of the most unbelievable engineering tasks ever undertaken by any railroad man in the history of the world.

Work Section

TRUE-FALSE

Answer the following questions true or false.
1. George Franklin Drew was the state's first Democratic governor after the Civil War.
2. Railroads were responsible for much of Florida's growth after the Civil War.
3. Railroads were closely regulated.
4. The National Convention of the Farmers Alliance met in Ocala in 1890.
5. The Ocala Demands came out of the Farmers Alliance convention.
6. Henry Bradley Plant worked for the Union Army during the Civil War.
7. Henry Morrison Flagler was a partner of John D. Rockefeller.
8. Winston Churchill was a war correspondent during the Spanish-American War.

MULTIPLE CHOICE

Only one of the following answers is correct. Select the right one.
1. Post-Civil War homestead lands were available first only to
   a. Southerners who had been loyal to the United States
   b. Northerners who migrated to Florida
   c. Freedmen
   d. All of the above

2. The first railroad commission in Florida was created by
   a. Gov. Edward A. Perry
   b. Henry Plant
   c. Henry Flagler
   d. Gen. Robert E. Lee

3. The Ocala Demands called for
   a. Unlimited coinage of silver
   b. Direct election of U.S. Senators
   c. Graduated income tax
   d. All of the above

4. Henry Plant was born in
   a. Georgia
   b. Connecticut
   c. New York
   d. Florida

5. The Tampa Bay Hotel was built by
   a. Henry Flagler
   b. Jefferson Davis
   c. Henry Plant
   d. Napoleon Broward

6. The Spanish-American War started after
   a. Plant built his railroad to Tampa
   b. The Ocala Demands had been published
   c. The battleship Maine blew up
   d. All of the above

7. The Rough Riders were led by
   a. Henry Plant
   b. Jefferson Davis
   c. Theodore Roosevelt
   d. Winston Churchill

8. Napoleon Bonaparte Broward was
   a. Governor of Florida
   b. Elected U.S. Senator from Florida
   c. Sheriff of Duval County
   d. All of the above

COMPLETION

Fill in the blanks in the following sentences with the correct word or phrase.
1. One of the first national farmers' organizations was

2. Henry Bradley Plant named his railroad

3. Henry Morrison Flagler named his

4. The first American troops bound for Cuba left from

5. Napoleon Bonaparte Broward was born in _____ County.

6. Broward's ship which ran the Cuban blockade was called

7. The governors who followed Broward in office were _____ and _____

8. Flagler completed his railroad to Key West in

SUGGESTED WORK PROJECTS

A. Using a map of Florida, locate the following places and tell why they were important.
   1. Ocala
   2. Perry
   3. Tampa
   4. St. Augustine
   5. Palm Beach
   6. Key West

B. Have students obtain a railroad map and trace the two main rail lines in Florida.

C. Where possible, plan field trips to
   1. The Flagler home in Palm Beach, now a museum
   2. Fernandina Island
   3. Tampa Bay Hotel
   4. The naval base at Key West

Part VIII
Twentieth Century
Florida

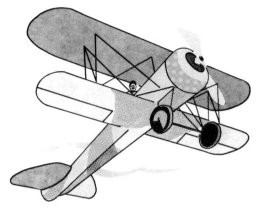

WORLD WAR I

On April 6, 1917, the Congress of the United States, answering a request from President Woodrow Wilson, declared the United States to be at war with Germany and her allies. Thus the United States entered what would later be called World War I.

While this country's participation in that war would last only 19 months, it would bring changes to Florida which, even today, have altered the entire outlook of the state.

For the first time in the history of warfare, the airplane became an important factor. Unlike other weapons of war, in order to train people to use the airplane, weather was an important factor. Flying schools were built throughout the south where ideal flying weather was available. No state answered the purpose better than Florida.

As a result, airfields were built in many parts of the state.

AVIATION

Five of the 35 flying schools in the United States were awarded to Florida. One was located at Pensacola, two at Miami and two at Arcadia.

The Pensacola Naval Air Station opened in 1914 with three instructors, 12 mechanics and nine seaplanes. In 1915, the station scored an important first by launching Lt. Cmdr. H. D. Martin and his aircraft from the deck of the USS North Carolina by means of a catapult. The action led to the development of aircraft carriers which played such a major part in World War II.

World War I began for many Floridians with this announcement in the April 6, 1917 issue of the Miami Herald.

By July 1, 1917, Pensacola had 45 instructors, 200 student flyers and more than 1,200 mechanics and, when the war ended in 1918, there were more than 400 officers and nearly 6,000 enlisted men there.

The other bases in Florida never reached numbers that large in their training programs but several hundred airmen did receive flying instructions at these four bases.

OTHER WARTIME ACTIVITIES

Because of Florida's long coastline, it also was necessary to station many other military and naval personnel in Florida.

Training camps for Army units sprang up near a number of Florida cities.

Three defensive sea area headquarters also were established with the main bases at Key West, Tampa and Pensacola.

And, because the state was surrounded by water and had a history of sea activities, ship building became an important part of the civilian contributions to the war effort.

Major shipyards were placed in operation in Jacksonville, Tampa and several other smaller cities around the state's coastline. Jacksonville built several ships of 3,500 tons and more, including two 7,500-ton concrete tankers. Tampa shipyards built more than 20 steel ships and several wooden cargo vessels. Many barges and smaller ships were built in shipyards along the state's Panhandle area.

PROHIBITION

While the country was at war, a constitutional amendment was proposed to prohibit the manufacture, sale and use of alcoholic beverages. When it was passed in 1919, the people of the U.S. referred to the new law as "Prohibition."

Again, because of its unique location and many miles of coastline, the Amendment meant a major role for the state during the Prohibition Era.

The many miles of the Florida Keys and the fact they were so close to Cuba and the Bahama Islands, where liquor could be obtained legally, made the state ideal for "Rum Runners" who wanted to smuggle that liquor into the United States illegally.

These law enforcement officers have just destroyed the still in the foreground. Why do you think prohibition failed in the United States?

Florida soon became one of the main highways for the illegal liquor traffic. Local law enforcement officials often were indifferent to this traffic. Enforcement of the Amendment was left largely to federal officials. There were too few of them so importation of illegal liquor quickly became a big business, leading to the growth of gangsterism throughout the nation and attracting many of them to Florida.

Soon it became necessary to call upon the Coast Guard to help out other federal agents and there were times it appeared Americans were waging war against each other.

DEATH AT SEA

For example, on August 7, 1927, Coast Guard cutter CG-249 hailed a motorboat while on patrol off the coast of Fort Lauderdale. When orders to stop were ignored, the boat fired several shots across the bow of the motorboat, and forced it to stop. The Coast Guard crew boarded her for a search. Crewmen found 160 cases of illegal liquor aboard.

The motorboat crew was placed under arrest and disarmed. But, one of the rum-runner's crew members was able to secure a gun after he had been searched. When he was transferred to the Coast Guard ship, he shot and killed its captain.

He then took the captain's gun and handed it to a second member of the outlaw crew. They then shot another Coast Guardsman and the radioman, as well.

The outlaws now had control of both ships and ordered all the Coast Guardsmen to return to the rum-runner, threatening to kill them if they didn't obey. The two outlaws then decided to blow up the Coast Guard cutter.

However, before they could accomplish this, two of the Coast Guardsmen jumped one of the armed men and overpowered him. The sound of that fight brought the second armed man racing back to help. The Coast Guardsmen were able to surprise him, however, and also disarm him. They then radioed to Fort Lauderdale and help was sent to the two ships.

In all, four men died in the fighting and two others were badly injured. The two outlaws eventually were brought to trial, convicted of the killings and sentenced to death.

The Growth of Aviation

Orville and Wilbur Wright introduced powered flight to the world on December 17, 1903, at Kittyhawk, N.C.

However, their invention was considered little more than a novelty until World War I was declared in 1914. Then, suddenly the aircraft became a major weapon of war. The importance of aircraft was discussed earlier in this chapter.

When peace returned to the world in 1918, development of the airplane continued at a fairly rapid pace in Europe. In the United States, however, interest was less widespread. Only a few pioneers continued to work at developing the aircraft as a means of transporting passengers and items (such as mail) in those early years.

Because Florida had been a leader in aviation during World War I and because its weather provided almost perfect conditions for the development of aviation, it also was near the head of the air flight parade in post-war years.

Some pioneers had come along even before the United States entered the war and among the most famous was Tony Jannus. Jannus started the first scheduled airline service in the country when he began making regular trips between St. Petersburg and Tampa. There were no bridges between the cities at that time.

The first of Jannus' trips was made on January 1, 1914, when he flew St. Petersburg mayor A. C. Pheil to Tampa. The mayor paid $400 for the honor of being the first passenger.

Soon Jannus was operating two flights each day and he continued that schedule for 187 days.

Post-war developments were more spectacular.

Eastern Airlines offered air travel for the hardy with this early plane. Seats were wooden chairs; cabins were not pressurized, heated, cooled, or insulated from noise of the engines. Do you think people would tolerate such comfortless travel today?

In 1927, Pan American Airlines came into being when regular flights were started between Key West and Cuba.

Eastern Airlines was born on January 1, 1931, when it established the first regular passenger service between Miami and New York. The airline used six-passenger Kingbirds for its service. By 1934, Capt. Eddie Rickenbacker, who had been America's ace of aces during World War I and was now president of Eastern, bought a group of DC-2 aircraft and began dawn-to-dusk flights between Miami and New York.

Also in 1934, National Airlines began operating, with its home base in St. Petersburg. Its first contract was a mail contract and connected St. Petersburg, Tampa, Lakeland, Orlando and Daytona Beach.

President of the National organization was a man named Ted Baker and, soon after he had won his mail contract, he added passenger service with 1935 Stinson aircraft.

Tony Jannus operated his airline briefly in 1914.

THE FLYERS

Florida produced its share of native-son flyers and one of the most famous in those early years was Albert Whitted.

Whitted was the son of Mr. and Mrs. T. A. Whitted, early residents of the city of St. Petersburg.

In 1917, the young man enlisted in the naval aviation corps and became one of the first 250 flyers graduated from that school. He was appointed chief instructor at Pensacola shortly after receiving his commission and was discharged from the Navy in 1919.

After his discharge, he bought a Bluebird aircraft and returned to St. Petersburg where he entered commercial aviation. During these days, he introduced literally hundreds of Floridians to flying. In 1921, he began building his own aircraft, named it the Falcon and, in the spring of 1922, he put it to commercial use.

On August 19, 1923, Whitted was engaged to pilot a charter flight for four people in Pensacola and, during the flight, his airplane ran into trouble. He crashed near Pensacola and he and all four of his passengers died in the accident.

DALE MABRY

Another of Florida's aviation pioneers also died in a crash early in his career.

Dale Mabry was one of Florida aviators to whom flying had become a way of life. He piloted lighter-than-air craft, such as balloons and dirigibles.

He was Capt. Dale Mabry.

Like Whitted, Mabry entered the flying service in 1917, during the war, and served in France as a member of the balloon corps of the American Expeditionary Forces (AEF).

After the war, Mabry decided to remain in the air service and on the morning of February 21, 1922, was serving as commander of the semi-rigid dirigible Roma.

The dirigible was used in Florida until the dangers of the craft were realized. What were some of these dangers? Here, the "Akron" floats over Miami Beach in 1933.

The Roma had been purchased from Italy and was filled with hydrogen gas.

Shortly after takeoff, it struck high-tension wires near Langley Field, Virginia, exploded in flames and crashed.

Of the 45 men aboard, 11 jumped to safety but Captain Mabry and 33 others died in the crash.

The Roaring Twenties

Despite disasters which claimed the lives of such pioneering men, aviation progressed rapidly in those years.

But, there was disaster of another kind in store for Florida during the twenties and it was of much greater proportion than any aircraft accident.

Florida's growth during the first half of the twenties was what was referred to as boom proportions.

The 1920 census revealed the state now had a population of 968,470 residents. Five years later, the count had risen to 1,263,540 and by 1930 it was almost 1.5 million.

Jacksonville, Miami and Tampa all enjoyed populations of more than 100,000 residents. Thirteen new counties were created in 1921, 1923 and 1925 and the majority of these were in the southern part of the state which had been very lightly populated until then.

The state's two main railroads had reached as far south as Naples on the Gulf Coast and Flagler had extended his line as far as Key West on the east coast.

The state was building hundreds of miles of new roads, connecting most of the main cities and even the Everglades was bridged with the opening of the Tamiami Trail in 1928.

The stage was set for one of the biggest booms in the country's history.

Unfortunately, disaster also was on the way.

PROSPERITY

With the opening of previously sparsely populated areas of the state, land sales began to skyrocket. Hundreds of speculators began buying up thousands of acres of land, then reselling those same acres at inflated prices the next day.

Millionaires were made overnight as prices continued to spiral upward in a frenzy of inflation.

All over the state, developers rented special buses bringing prospective buyers into the state and sold building lots by the hundreds.

D. P. "Doc" Davis, for example, developed Davis Islands in Tampa and sold 300 lots in one day for a total of nearly $1.7-million. Before the end of 1925, he had sold his entire development for more than $18-million.

But, such a boom was certain to be followed by problems.

A land development auction in Miami, 1923. Here fortunes were made and lost every day.

The demand for housing was immense. Soon rents were so high the average person could not afford them. The demand for building materials put such a strain on railroads and shipping that their ability to transport these materials could not keep up.

People who had flocked to Florida became more and more disappointed at their inability to get needed materials and began to write those back north about the impossible problems they were faced with.

Newspapers soon became aware of the situation in Florida and began writing stories advising prospective Florida residents to stay away from the state.

Land sales then began to fall off. Inflated prices began returning to something nearer normal levels and millionaires, who had made their fortunes overnight, began to lose them just as quickly.

THE BUST

Now, nature stepped in to take a hand and hasten disaster.

On September 19, 1926, a hurricane roared ashore at Miami. Before it blew itself out, nearly 400 persons were dead, more than 6,000 injured and thousands more had suffered huge property losses.

The bad publicity, added to what already had happened to Florida's image in northern newspapers, was the final blow which killed the boom.

But, disaster was to add yet another blow. On September 16, 1928, another hurricane rushed ashore. This one plunged inland from Palm Beach with winds of more than 130 miles per hour, slammed into the Lake Okeechobee area, and forced water out of the lake, flooding the surrounding countryside.

69

Banks all over Florida closed as people panicked and withdrew their money. How would you feel if you saw a line like this in front of a bank where you had your life savings?

No one knows precisely how many lives were lost in that disastrous storm but Red Cross officials feel the dead numbered more than 2,000 before it was over.

Several weeks later, a major freeze struck the state, wiping out many crops and almost completely destroying the citrus crop.

Florida, a boom state just three years earlier, was now rocked back on its heels, suffering from a series of man-made and natural disasters which painted a grim picture for the rest of the country.

DEPRESSION

The Great Depression for almost all of the United States was preceded by the stock market crash of October 1929.

In Florida, however, it actually began three years earlier with the collapse of the land boom we have just discussed.

As early as 1926, as many as 40 banks were forced to close in Florida, although many were to reorganize and reopen at later dates.

But, between 1925 and 1932, 45 national banks and 171 state banks collapsed as national problems piled upon those problems already gripping Florida.

In 1929, Doyle Carlton became Florida's governor and he found state finances in miserable condition. Looking around for means to raise more money for state use, the Legislature legalized parimutuel betting at horse and dog tracks throughout the state. It also added a penny to state gasoline taxes.

But, despite these added revenues, conditions failed to improve much and the state followed the rest of the country into deep depression. Many counties and cities were forced to adopt welfare programs.

RECOVERY

In 1932, the nation turned to Franklin D. Roosevelt as President to help it out of the depression which gripped the country. The same year, Floridians elected David Sholtz as governor.

When Sholtz took office, the depression was in its worst stages. The annual per capita income in Florida was down to $289.

Sholtz tried hard to pull the state out of its problems. He even asked for a loan, backed by the state's credit pledge, but the Supreme Court ruled against him.

As 1933 continued, however, some of the national programs started by President Roosevelt began to find their way into the state and projects such as the Civilian Conservation Corps, Works Project Administration and

Civil Works Administration began putting people back to work.

In 1935, President Roosevelt announced that $5-million would be allocated to a Cross-Florida Barge Canal, a project which still causes a great deal of argument in the state although it has been stopped.

As such programs began to take hold, pumping new money into the state, recovery slowly began.

But, the return of true prosperity did not take place until 1941 and then was fueled only by the start of another war.

Florida in World War II

In 1939, Germany attacked Poland and World War II gripped Europe. Before it ended in 1945, the United States was drawn into the conflict and the last signs of a lingering depression evaporated in a wartime economy.

Florida was to witness as much of the war as any, and more than most, of the states.

The increase in defense activities actually was felt even before this country entered the war itself in December 1941. Thousands of service men came to the state to man new bases in almost every corner of Florida.

There was a new naval air station at Jacksonville, an Army training center at Camp Blanding, a reactivated naval base at Key West, Drew and MacDill air stations in Tampa, Eglin air station at Valparaiso and increased activities at many of the older bases.

The Air Force took over more than 70,000 hotel rooms in Miami and Miami Beach to expand training facilities there. Elsewhere in the state, other training schools shot up almost overnight.

But, Florida's contributions to the war effort were not limited to its military bases. Ship building became a major industry. Agricultural products were grown everywhere in the state and thousands of tons of foodstuffs were shipped elsewhere to help out the war effort.

When the United States entered the war in 1941, activities picked up even more. Coastal and anti-submarine patrol stations were opened at many points around the state's shorelines. Even lighter-than-air craft were pressed into action.

While Florida supplied fewer than 50,000 men to the armed forces in World War I, during World War II, more than 250,000 Floridians, both men and women, were called into uniform.

CLOAK AND DAGGER

Florida even was the scene of one of the most unusual spy stories which took place during the war. On June 18, 1942, four German spies landed from a submarine at Ponte Vedra Beach, dressed in American civilian clothes and carrying forged papers and nearly $200,000 in cash and bonds. They also carried incendiary pens and pencils with which they intended to damage U.S. war industries.

Another group of German spies also landed on Long Island, N.Y. One of that number turned informer and told the Federal Bureau of Investigation (FBI) about the Florida landings and the men involved.

After the Florida group landed, they took a bus to Jacksonville, where they split up. Two went on to Chicago, two to New York City. All eventually were captured before they could carry out their missions.

In short, Florida was an extremely busy and prosperous state during World War II. There were those who feared, when peace came in 1945, that the state would slip back into the bust period as the country readjusted to post-war living and a reduced economy.

Mary Bethune, a pioneer in black education, served as the director of the Division of Negro Affairs from 1936 to 1945. She founded the Daytona Literary and Industrial School for Training Negro Girls, which later merged with the Cookman Institute, forming Bethune-Cookman College.

THE POST-WAR YEARS

As it developed, nothing could have been further from the truth. Instead of another bust, the state began its greatest period of growth.

What were the reasons?

Many people felt a large part of Florida's new popularity was caused by the favorable impression the balmy weather had made on thousands of servicemen who were stationed in the state during the just completed war.

But, that factor by itself could not have accounted for the almost unbelievable increase in new residents. There were other factors, such as the booming post-war economy. Improved incomes and more leisure time brought millions of vacationing tourists to the Sunshine State. In turn, as many of them reached retirement age, they began to consider leaving colder climates to seek more pleasant year-round weather in which to spend their years of freedom. Florida was a ready answer.

48 states that then made up this nation, it ranked in the bottom half in size — 27th.

Ten years later — the war now behind us — the trend toward more rapid growth was becoming very evident to everyone. By 1950, the number of residents who called Florida home had risen to nearly three million, and the state had moved into the top half on the nation's population list, reaching number 20. To the more optimistic, the signal was that this was just the beginning of possibly the biggest boom of all.

Once again, it was the optimists who were right. The national census-takers made their rounds again in 1960 and, when all the figures had been added up, even the optimists felt an error might have been made. Those figures showed that Florida now had nearly five-million residents and it had jumped all the way up to 10th on the list which ranked states according to total population.

By now, the biggest portion felt that five million might be the end of the upswing but, when the census

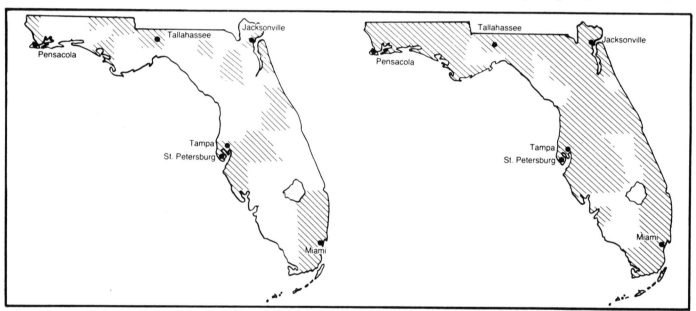

Florida's growth from 1940 (left) to 1950 (right). The shaded areas represent counties with more than 25 people per square mile. What areas of Florida grew fastest?

Also, adding significantly to these two items was a third — the nation's space program, a large portion of which became centered in Florida, beginning in the mid-1950s.

Taken as a package, the results produced by far the greatest population boom the Sunshine State ever had witnessed.

FANTASTIC GROWTH

When the Federal government took the 1940 Census, Florida had slightly more than two-million people within its state boundaries. And, among the

was taken again in 1970, it was evident the boom had stretched through another ten years. Florida climbed one more rung on the ladder measuring state sizes to 9th when nearly two-million more people chose to make their homes in the Sunshine State and the population soared to nearly seven million.

TOURISM

Was Florida's reputation for mild and pleasant year-round weather alone enough to cause so many people to choose Florida as their home? There is little doubt but what it had much to do with many decisions. But, one must list a number of other attractions which brought travelers here in the first place.

Attractions?

Yes! Along with natural wonders the weathermen continues to supply, the decade of the 1970s also produced a growing number of man-made marvels which acted as an even greater magnet for tourists.

And, there was a reason for such industrious building. Just as Florida's population growth left many people wondering where it would all end, individual incomes in the United States jumped almost as rapidly. In the years immediately after the end of World War II, the average working person in this nation earned about $1500 per year. Twenty years later, that average was almost four times as great. As a result of increased incomes, travel became one of the largest businesses in the country. The business is generally called Tourism and Florida soon was enjoying more than a normal share of these vacation dollars.

Some of the most recent figures, coming from the experts in Tallahassee, show just how important tourism has become within our state. For example, in 1979, more than 35-million people visited Florida. On the average, they stayed nearly two weeks and, during that time, they spent almost $500 each while visiting the many parks, beaches, and man-made attractions the Sunshine State has to offer. During the year that we are examining, those tourists spent nearly $16-billion in Florida.

MAN-MADE ATTRACTIONS

That is a lot of money! And, because it is, it has brought a large number of huge entertainment parks to the state within the last ten years.

Many have been centered in the Orlando area and the first that comes to mind, of course, is Walt Disney World, a 28,000-acre site that includes something for nearly everyone of any age. In its first ten years (it opened for business in 1971), this huge park attracted more than 140-million guests. In 1982, a new addition was opened, and the EPCOT Center (Experimental Prototype Community of Tomorrow), it is predicted, will attract even larger numbers than does the Magic Kingdom. Walt Disney World has invested slightly less than $2-billion in its huge park and provides jobs for several hundred employees.

However, this sprawling center is only one of a number that have opened or expanded from smaller efforts throughout Florida in recent years. Admittedly, it is the largest and most lavish, but dozens of others provide a wide variety of other types of entertainment, such as Tampa's Busch Gardens and Sea World, also near Orlando. Dozens of other historical displays and educational museums also are visited by thousands of guests in almost every corner of the Sunshine State.

When you combine the abilities of man to build such a variety of attractions with the natural wonders of Florida, you have an almost irresistible lure.

The Space Age

Now let's return to the realm of flight. As you recall from our explorations earlier in this chapter, Florida and Floridians were very active during the early years of aviation development. But, all of those contributions to the age of flight, while extremely important in the pioneer years, must be classified as minor since the space age moved into the center of the skies during the last half of our present century.

For example, early in 1950, construction began on a long-range missile testing base at Cape Canaveral on the state's Atlantic coast. During World War II, that site had been known as the Banana River Naval Air Station. Now the name was changed to Patrick Air Force Base and new, different, and more complicated activities soon were underway at the revitalized and renamed station.

On July 24, 1950, the first missile test was made from there, and the site has been the home of innumerable firsts from that day to the present.

Consider that America's first man in space, Alan Shepard, was launched from Cape Canaveral on May 5, 1961. His trip did not take him into orbit, even though it took him into space.

However, just slightly more than nine months later, on February 20, 1962, John Glenn, who has since become a United States senator, became the first American to go into orbit, sailing three times around the earth. With his feat, a new term was born that, in succeeding years, has become very familiar to us all. The United States had its "astronauts."

What that breed of men — and now women —

Apollo II astronaut stands beside U.S. flag on the moon.

has accomplished over the years continues to amaze the world and, without exception, all of their trips into space have originated right here in Florida.

Let's review, just to sample a few, the contributions Florida has made to the nation's space program.

PROJECT MERCURY

Those first tentative steps into manned space flight, the flights which included Shepard's and Glenn's contributions, were known as Project Mercury. The capsules used in the program were very small units which allowed only one man at a time to occupy them. Consequently, accomplishments were basic, but the program was truly pioneer in nature and, because that was its aim, it fulfilled its role and opened the way to much larger units and more complicated flights and experiments.

The climax of the program was reached when MA-9 was launched on May 15, 1963, with Astronaut L. Gordon Cooper aboard. Before the flight was completed, just slightly more than 34 hours later, Cooper had spun twenty-two orbital passes around the earth and the nation's space scientists knew they had laid a firm foundation and were ready to take the next big step outward.

GEMINI PROGRAM

That next big step was called the Gemini program, built around larger and more complex spacecraft that would accommodate two astronauts, side by side. The program's primary objectives were to extend the length of space flights; to meet and dock with another space vehicle while in flight; and to test man outside his spaceship on space walks. Of course, there also were dozens of other technical tests and experiments included in the program.

As in the case of Mercury, all of the Gemini objectives were successfully completed and a number of additional firsts in space were recorded during the program. Among the most important came during the flight of Gemini IV, flown by James McDivitt and Edward H. White III. White became the first man in history to leave his craft in space and operate at the end of a tether, proving man could do chores outside his spacecraft.

Less than a year later, the astronauts on Gemini VIII scored another space first when Neil A. Armstrong and David R. Scott performed the first in-space docking with another space vehicle.

The entire Gemini program was to last through twelve flights and, like Mercury, open a multitude of new roads that would lead the nation even deeper into space.

APOLLO PROGRAM

During the Gemini program, astronauts Frank Borman and James Lovell set a record of fourteen days in space, more than 330 hours in flight. It proved that men could stay in space, without ill effects, long enough to travel to the moon and back. The Apollo program — third in NASA's manned-space series — was designed to bring that dream to life.

Apollo 8 was the first to actually reach the vicinity of the moon. William Anders joined Borman and Lovell, the men from the Gemini endurance flight, to achieve that honor. Two more flights followed, during one of which the Lunar Module was tested in flight and, on the second, descent was made to within 8.5 miles of the moon's surface.

That preparation set the stage for the magic man-on-the-moon accomplishment promised by President John F. Kennedy soon after his inauguration. Apollo 11 lifted off from Cape Canaveral on July 16, 1969, and, four days later, deposited Neil Armstrong and Edwin Aldrin on the moon, while Mike Collins orbited above them. Armstrong was first to leave the module and, as he stepped upon the moon's surface, television viewers on earth heard him comment, "That's one small step for man, one giant leap for mankind."

Additional visits to the moon followed before the National Aeronautics and Space Administration changed programs once again. This time, the "capsule" became a huge spaceship.

SPACE SHUTTLE

As the nation's space program moved into the decade of the 1980s, concentration was directed toward extended space shuttle operations, what NASA described as a "new era in space travel."

The vehicle — larger than many commercial aircraft — is launched into space like a rocket, flown in orbit like a spacecraft, and landed like an airplane. The re-usable orbiter vehicle has an undetermined life-span. Many shuttle missions have been flown, and their successes promise to lead the nation into ever broader aspects of space travel and ever new wonders for Florida's historic Cape Canaveral.*

*The name was changed to Cape Kennedy in the early days of the space program. Later, it was changed back to Canaveral, and now the Kennedy Space Center is located at Cape Canaveral.

With astronauts Young and Crippen at the controls, *Columbia* touches down on dry-lake runway at Edwards Air Force Base. This perfect landing epitomized the space shuttle's performance, which exceeded expectations throughout the mission.

Summary: Florida Today

Allen Morris, who compiles the popular state publication entitled *The Florida Handbook,* recently observed that Florida has become "one of the super-states of the United States."

The observation couldn't be more correct.

Let's look at some of the facts. The 1980 Census, the latest official figures which describe so many aspects of American life, show that the state of Florida now has reached 9,739,992 in population. Unofficially, it probably now exceeds 10 million, as newcomers are flooding in at a rate of nearly 9,000 every day.

That has moved Florida up to 7th on the list of largest states in the nation, and means its voting power in the Congress of the United States is a major factor in determining the laws under which we are governed at the national level.

Although tourism and its related services rate as Florida's chief source of income, the economy of the state is much more balanced than many outsiders recognize.

Consider the citrus industry. Recent predictions indicate that before the 1980s have ended, Florida growers will be producing more than 210-million boxes of citrus fruit annually. The production of oranges and grapefruit alone during the 1979-80 growing season accounted for almost 75 percent of all commercial citrus fruits grown in the nation. Moreover, the production of frozen concentrated orange juice within the state represented more than 90 percent of all that product available throughout the United States.

And there are other significant commercial ventures. Florida's phosphate mines are the largest in the country. The state also rates high in the production of garden vegetables and livestock. It has a booming lumber industry and even ranks among the nation's top ten in oil production. Its commercial fishing industry produces millions of additional dollars.

TRANSPORTATION

Fortunately for the state's industrialists and for the wealth of tourists who visit here, Florida's transportation system has kept pace with growth.

There are, for example, fourteen air carrier airports which service more than 25-million passengers annually, many of them bound for foreign nations. Additionally, dozens of private airports exist across the state. The highway system is among the most modern in the country, and the extent of Florida's interstate system is well above the national average. All told, the state boasts nearly 100,000 miles of public roads. Several major seaports are busy all around Florida's 8,000 miles of coastline, and major railroads operate over more than 6,000 miles of track.

EDUCATION

For many years, the state's educational system lagged badly behind much of the rest of the nation, but in recent years that outlook has changed significantly. Currently, more than 1.5-million students attend public schools in the K-12 category. Another quarter-million attend private schools and, together, they graduate nearly 100,000 annually from high school.

Florida also boasts a state university system that accommodates approximately 130,000 students and has another 27 degree-granting colleges and universities, plus 28 public community colleges. The Sunshine State was the first in the nation to complete a long-range plan to provide community college education to all of its citizens, and currently, more than 95 percent of the state's population is within commuting distance of a community college.

Less than fifty years ago, Florida was a largely rural state that lagged badly behind much of the rest of the nation in many aspects of daily life. That picture has changed dramatically, and, as Allen Morris has described it, Florida now is one of the nation's superstates.

RECENT GOVERNORS

Much of that progress has been made during the last twenty years or less, and the State of Florida has been fortunate to have two young and progressive men lead it during that period of its greatest growth.

Florida's 37th governor was Reubin O'Donovan Askew, who was elected in 1970 and took office in January of the following year. Only 42 years old when he assumed the job, the Pensacola resident proved a most able administrator and succeeded in winning tax reform, increasing homestead exemptions for the elderly and disabled, and upgrading the school system. He brought Florida directly into the national political spotlight by delivering the Keynote Address at the 1972 Democratic National Convention and, after he left office following two successful terms, he became the United States Trade Representative, with Cabinet-level rank, under President Jimmy Carter.

Governor Askew was succeeded by a native Floridian, Daniel Robert Graham, who also was 42 when he moved into the governor's mansion in Tallahassee. Unlike Askew, however, Graham was a complete product of modern Florida. Born in Coral Gables in 1936, Bob Graham was educated in the state public school system and received his initial higher education at the University of Florida. He later earned his law degree at Harvard, but immediately returned to his home state and, in 1966, was elected to the State Legislature.

Again, Graham brought reform to Tallahassee when he assumed the governorship and was the first to preside over biennial budgeting. Many additional improvements followed, including a blanket increase in homestead exemptions, one of the five constitutional amendments that he proposed, and the voters approved his first term in office. Graham was re-elected in 1982.

Florida's history, as compared to many of the other states in the nation, is comparatively brief and her discovery by the rest of the residents of this country is comparatively recent. But the awakened giant obviously has emerged from a long sleep and its future may be limited only by her boundaries.

The state's history to date has been a series of ups and downs. Since the end of World War II, however, the down cycles appear to have ended. The future may be ever upward.

Work Section

TRUE-FALSE

Answer the following questions true or false.
1. The Pensacola Naval Air Station opened in 1914.
2. It was the only military base in Florida during World War I.
3. Tony Jannus started the first regularly scheduled airline service in the United States.
4. National Airlines was founded in Florida.
5. Dale Mabry was killed in the crash of a dirigible.
6. The end of the Florida boom came in 1932.
7. Four German spies landed in Florida in 1942 and never were captured.
8. Florida's population had reached five million by 1940.
9. Alan Shepard was the first U.S. astronaut launched from Cape Kennedy.
10. Florida now has more than 10-million residents.

MULTIPLE CHOICE

Only one of the following answers is correct. Select the right one.
1. The first man to be launched in an aircraft from the deck of a ship was
   a. Tony Jannus
   b. Dale Mabry
   c. Lt. Cmdr. H. D. Martin
   d. Albert Whitted

2. Major shipyards were in operation during World War I in
   a. Jacksonville
   b. Tampa
   c. Both of the above

3. Ships which brought illegal liquor into the United States during prohibition were known as
   a. Rum runners
   b. Coast Guard cutters
   c. Cargo ships
   d. None of the above

4. The first passenger on a regularly scheduled airplane flight in the United States was
   a. Tony Jannus
   b. A. C. Pheil
   c. David Sholtz
   d. Doyle Carlton

5. The Tamiami Trail opened in
   a. 1914
   b. 1919
   c. 1924
   d. 1928

6. More than 2,000 people died in the hurricane of
   a. 1914
   b. 1919
   c. 1926
   d. 1928

7. The first money appropriated for the Cross-Florida Barge Canal was in
   a. 1935
   b. 1941
   c. 1952
   d. None of the above

8. The first missile was tested at Cape Canaveral in
   a. 1949
   b. 1952
   c. 1961
   d. None of the above

9. The first man to make an orbital flight in space from Cape Canaveral was
   a. Alan Shepard
   b. John Glenn
   c. A. C. Pheil
   d. Albert Whitted

10. In 1960, Florida's population was approximately
    a. 10 million
    b. 4 million
    c. 5 million
    d. 7 million

11. The state's largest business is
    a. tourism
    b. space
    c. aviation
    d. ship building

COMPLETION

Fill in the blanks in the following sentences with the correct word or phrase.

1. _____ of the 35 flying schools in the United States during World War I were in Florida.

2. In World War I, three defensive sea headquarters were established in Key West, Tampa and _____

3. Prohibition was established by a _____

4. _____ airlines were founded in the state of Florida.

5. In 1920, three Florida cities had more than 100,000 population. They were Jacksonville, Miami and _____

6. During World War II, two air bases were established in Tampa. They were. _____ and _____

7. The German spies who landed in Florida came ashore from a _____

8. During the depression, the per capita income in Florida was less than _____

9. The Air Force used more than _____ hotel rooms in Miami and Miami Beach during World War II.

10. The flight which landed the first men on the moon was a mission in the _____ series.

SUGGESTED WORK PROJECTS

1. If possible take classes on a field trip to any of the following places in the state.
   a. The Naval Air Museum in Pensacola
   b. Cape Kennedy
   c. Albert Whitted Airport in St. Petersburg
   d. MacDill Field in Tampa
   e. Eglin Air Force Base in Valparaiso

Index

Adams-Onis Treaty, 35, 36
Africa, 31
Akron (dirigible), 68
Alabama, 7, 47
Alabama River, 32
Alachua, 1, 53
Alachua County, 44
Alafia, 1
Albert Whitted Airport, 74
Aldrin, Edwin, 75
Altamaha River, 15, 16
Amrister, Robert Christie, 34, 36
Amelia Island, 33, 36, 37
America, Central, 1
America, North, 2, 3, 6, 8, 17, 18, 22, 24
America, South, 1, 4, 5
American Expeditionary Forces (AEF), 68
Ames, Henry, 59
Anders, William, 75
Apalachee, 4, 5, 13, 18
Apalachee Indians, 2
Apalachicola, 1
Apalachicola River, 6, 9, 22, 27, 32, 33, 36
Apollo Program, 75
Apopka, 1
Apoxsee, 1
Arbuthnot, Alexander, 34, 36
Arcadia, Fla. 65
Armstrong, Neil, 74
Asia, 1
Askew, Reubin, 76
Atlantic Ocean, 5
Attractions, 73
Augusta, Ga., 59
Aury, Luis, 33, 36
Austria, 15, 18

Bahama Islands, 29, 31, 66
Baker, Ted, 67
Ballast Point, 49
Banana River Naval Air Station, 73
Baton Rouge, La., 31
Bell, John, 47
Bethune, Mary McLeod, 71
Bimini, 2, 3
Bithlo, 1
Black Codes, 52, 55
Bluebird (airplane), 68
Boca Ciega Bay, 8
Bolivar, Simon, 33
Booth, John Wilkes, 51

Borman, Frank, 75
Bowles, William Augustus, 30, 31, 36
Brackenridge, John, 47
British Battalion, Third, 21
British Regiment, First, 21
British Regiment, Ninth, 21
British Regiment, 60th, 21
Brockenbaugh, William, 43
Broome, James, 44, 45
Broward Era, 62
Broward, Napoleon Bonaparte, 62
Brown, Thomas, 44
Busch Gardens, 73
Bushnell, 45
Butler, Robert, 35, 40

Cabell, Edward, 43, 44
Cabots (explorers), 2
Call, Richard Keith, 40, 42, 43, 45
Callava, Jose, 35
Caloosahatchee, 1
Calusa Indians, 2, 3, 8
Camp Blanding, 71
Canada, 7
Cape Canaveral, 2, 73, 75
Cape Kennedy, 75, 78
Caribbean, 3
Carlton, Doyle, 70, 77
Carter, Jimmy, 76
Castillo de San Marcos, 12, 17, 19, 22, 25, 27
Cedar Key, 51, 56
CG-249 (ship), 66
Charles V, King of Spain, 4
Charles Town, S.C., 11, 12, 18
Charleston, S.C., 30
Charlotte Harbor, 40
Chassahowitzka, 1
Chattachoochee, 1, 48
Chattachoochee River, 22, 27
Cherokee Indians, 22
Chicago, Ill., 71
Chickasaw Indians, 30
Choctaw Indians, 30
Chuluota, 1
Churchill, Winston, 61, 63
Citrus Industry, 76
Civil War, 49, 50, 54-57, 59, 60, 63
Civil Works Administration, 71
Civilian Conservation Corps (CCC), 70
Coacoochee (Wild Cat), 41, 42, 45
Coast Guard, 66

Collins, Mike, 75
Columbine (ship), 49
Columbus, Christopher, 2
Columbus, Diego, 3
Compromise of 1850, 44
Confederate States of America, 48, 56
Connecticut, 59, 63
Constitutional Amendment, 13th, 52
Constitutional Amendment, 14th, 52, 56
Constitutional Amendment, 18th, 66
Cooper, L. Gordon, 74
Cortez, Hernando, 3, 9
Creek Indians, 30
Crippen, Robert, 75
Cross-Florida Barge Canal, 71, 77, 78
Cuba, 15-18, 21, 23, 24, 26, 31, 60-63, 66, 67
Cuba, Bishop of, 6

Dade, Francis, 41
Dade Massacre, 41, 45
Darien, S.C., 15
Dartmouth College, 53
Davis, D. P. "Doc", 69
Davis Islands, 69
Davis, Jefferson, 48, 59
Daytona Beach, 67
DC-2 (airplane), 67
de Coligny, Gaspard, 5
de Galvez, Bernardo, 24, 25, 27
de Laudonniere, Rene Goulaine, 5, 6
de Luna, Tristan, 5, 6, 8
de Soto, Hernando, 4, 5, 8
de Vaca, Cabeza, 4
de Zespedes, Manuel, 25, 29, 36
Declaration of Independence, 24, 25, 27
Democratic Party, 54, 57
Diaz, Don Bentura, 21, 26, 27
Dickison, John J., 49, 50, 55
Disney World, 73
Dixieland, 50
Douglas, Stephen, 47
Drew, George Franklin, 57, 63
Dry Tortugas, 51
Duval County, 61, 62
Duval, William Pope, 35, 37, 39, 42, 44, 45

East River, 50
Eastern Airlines, 67
Econfina, 1
Edwards Air Force Base, 75
Eglin Air Force Base, 71, 78
Egmont Key, 48
Emancipation Proclamation, 51, 57
England, 15, 17-19, 22-26, 29-32, 36, 40, 61
EPCOT, 73

Escambia County, 35
Europe, 2, 3, 8, 15-17, 24, 71
Everglades, 41, 42, 69
Evergreen Cemetery, 50

Falcon (airplane), 68
Farmers Alliance, 59, 63
Farnese, Elizabeth, 15
Federal Bureau of Investigation (FBI), 71
Fenholloway, 1
Fernandina, 61
Finegan, Joseph, 49
Flagler, Henry Morrison, 59-63, 69
Florida Agricultural College, 54
Florida, East, 22-27, 42
Florida East Coast Railway, 59, 60, 62, 63
Florida Keys, 66
Florida, West, 22-27, 31, 32, 42
Fort Brooke, 41, 48, 56
Fort Caroline, 5, 8, 9
Fort Gadsden, 37
Fort Jefferson, 51, 56
Fort King, 41, 45
Fort King George, 15
Fort Lauderdale, 66
Fort Marion, 41
Fort Mims, 32
Fort Moultrie, 41
Fort Picolata, 16, 18
Fort Pupa, 16, 18
Fort San Carlos de Austria, 14
Fort San Marcos de Apalache, 14, 18, 19, 21, 22, 26, 27
Fountain of Youth, 3, 8
France, 5, 15, 17, 18, 24, 26
Franck, Jaime, 14, 18
French and Indian War, 17

Gadsden, James, 41
Gadsden Point, 48
Gaines, Edmund, 33
Gamble Mansion, 56
Georgia, 5, 6, 16-18, 25, 29-34, 51, 59, 63
Gemini Program, 74, 75
Germany, 71
Gibbs High School, 53
Gibbs, Jonathan, 53, 55
Gilchrist, Albert, 62
Glenn, John, 73, 74
Gold Coast, 61, 72
Graham, Robert, 77
Grand Banks, 62
Grant, James, 22, 23, 26, 27
Great Depression, 70
Great Lakes, 17

Greece, 23
Green Flag of Florida, 33, 36
Gulf of Mexico, 7, 14

Hart, Ossian B., 53
Harries, John, 22, 26, 27
Havana, 15, 18, 21, 29, 31, 60, 63
Hedges, John, 21, 26
Hernandez, Joseph, 41
Heyward, Thomas, 25, 27
Hialeah, 1
Hickpochee, 1
Hillsborough River, 48
Hispaniola, 2
Holland, 15, 18
Homosassa, 1
Homosassa Springs, 56
Horseshoe Bend, 32, 36
Hypoluxo, 1

Iamonia, 1
Immokalee, 1
Indian River, 23, 31
Indian Territory, 42
Istachatta, 1
Istokpoga, 1
Italy, 15, 23, 68

Jackson, Andrew, 32-37, 45
Jacksonville, 9, 18, 49, 50, 53, 60-62, 65, 69, 77
Jamestown, Va., 11, 18
Jannus, Tony, 67, 77
Jefferson County, 43
Jesup, Thomas, 41
Johnstone, George, 23, 26, 27
Jordan, Juan, 7, 9

Kennedy, Cape, 75
Kennedy, John F., 75
Kentucky, 35
Key Biscayne, 41
Key West, 9, 48, 60-63, 65-67, 69, 71, 78
Kindelan, Sebastian, 32
King George's War, 18
King Philip, 41, 42
Kingbirds (airplanes), 67
Kittyhawk, N.C., 67

Ladies Military Aid Organization, 51, 55
Lake City, 49
Lake George, 31
Lake Okeechobee, 69
Lakeland, 67
Langley Field, 68
Lee, Robert E., 59, 63

Le Moyne, Jean Baptiste, 15, 18
Levy, David (Yulee), 43, 45
Lincoln, Abraham, 44, 45, 47, 48, 51, 55
Lochloosa, 1
Lokossee, 1
Long Island, 71
Louisiana, 31
Loxahatchee, 1

Mabry, Dale, 68, 77
MacDill Air Force Base, 71, 78
Madison, Fla. 48
Madison, James, 32, 36
Marion Light Artillery, 49
Martin, H.D., 65, 77
Marvin, William, 55
Massachusetts, 11, 18, 24
Mathews, George, 32
McDivitt, 74
McGillivray, Alexander, 30, 36
McGillivray, Lachlan, 30
McGirt, Daniel, 29, 36
McGregor, George, 33, 34, 36
McKay, James, 48, 49
Mediterranean Sea, 23
Menendez, Pedro de Aviles, 6, 8, 27
Mercury, Project, 74
Mexico, 3-5, 7, 9, 33
Miami, 1, 61-63, 65, 67, 69, 71, 78
Miami Beach, 68, 71, 87
Miami Herald, 65
Micanopy, 1
Middleton, Arthur, 25, 27
Minorca, 23
Mississippi River, 5, 7, 17, 22, 24
Mobile, Ala., 7, 15, 18, 23, 24, 26, 27, 35
Mobile River, 14
Monroe, James, 33-36
Montgomery, Ala., 47
Moore, James, 13-18
Moosa, 15
Morris, Allen, 76
Moseley, William Dunn, 43, 45
Moultrie Creek, Treaty of, 40, 41, 45
Moultrie, John, 24, 26
Mudd, Samuel, 51

Naples, 69
Narvaez, Panfilo de, 3-5, 8, 9
Nashville, Tenn., 35
National Airlines, 67, 73
National Grange, 59
Natural Bridge, Battle of, 50
Naval Air Museum, 78
New Orleans, La., 15, 18, 24, 26, 27, 33

New Smyrna, 23, 24, 26, 27
New Spain, 3-5, 14
New York, 30, 59, 60, 63, 67, 71
New York, Treaty of, 30
Newfoundland, 62
Niblack, Silas L., 53
North Carolina, 67
Northwest Ordinance, 35

Ocala, 1, 40, 45, 49, 50, 56, 59, 63
Ocala Banner, 50
Ocala Demands, 59, 63
Ochlockonee, 1, 50
Ochopee, 1
Ochuse Bay, 5, 7, 8
Ogilvie, Francis, 21, 26
Oglethorpe, James, 16-18
Ohio River, 17
Okahumpka, 1
Okaloosa, 1
Okeechobee, 1
Oklahoma, 42
Oklawaha, 1, 58
Oklawaha River, 40
Olustee, Battle of, 49, 55, 56
Opalockee, 1
Orlando, Fla., 67, 72
Ortiz, Juan, 4, 5, 8
Osceola, 1, 41, 42, 45

Pahokee, 1
Palatka, 1, 49, 56
Palm Beach, 61, 63, 69
Palmer, John, 15, 18
Pan American Airlines, 67
Panama Canal, 63
Panama City, Fla., 72
Panasoffkee, 1
Panhandle, 2, 6, 9, 66
Panton Leslie and Co., 30, 36
Pascua Florida (Feast of Flowers), 3, 9
Patrick Air Force Base, 73
Paynes Landing, 40, 41, 45
Peace of Paris, 17
Pennawa, 1
Pensacola, 7-9, 14, 15, 17-19, 21-27, 30, 32-35,
    37, 39, 47, 48, 56, 65, 66, 68, 77
Pensacola Bay, 5, 7, 9
Pensacola Naval Air Station, 65
Perry, Edward A., 63
Perry, Madison Starke, 44, 45
Peru, 8
Pheil, A.C., 67, 77
Philadelphia, Pa., 53
Philip II, King of Spain, 6, 15

Philippine Islands, 17, 18
Phosphate, 76
Pizarro, Francisco, 4
Plant, Henry Bradley, 59-61, 63
Plant Investment Co., 60
Plymouth, Mass., 11, 18
Poland, 71
Ponce de Leon, Juan, 2-4, 8
Ponce de Leon Hotel, 60
Ponte Vedra Beach, 71
Population Growth, 72, 76
Populist Revolt, 58
Port St. Joe, 55
Prevost, Augustin, 21, 26
Princeton University, 53
Prohibition Era, 66
Puerto Rico, 2, 3
Putnam, Benjamin A., 43, 45

Quincy Guard, 48

Reconstruction Period, 54-56, 63
Red Cross, 70
Reed, Harrison, 53
Reid, Robert Raymond, 42, 45
Republican Party, 54
Revolutionary War, 18, 24, 26, 30
Ribault, Jean, 5
Richmond, Va., 51
Rickenbacker, Eddie, 67
Roanoke Island, N.C., 18
Rockefeller, Andrews and Flagler, 60
Rockefeller, John D., 60, 63
Roma (dirigible), 68
Roosevelt, Franklin D., 70, 71
Roosevelt, Theodore, 60
Rough Riders, 61
Rum Runners, 66, 77
Rutledge, Edward, 25, 27

Sabine River, 35
St. Augustine, 3, 6-9, 11-13, 15-18, 21-27, 29, 32,
    35, 37, 39-41, 47, 56, 60
St. Johns County, 35
St. Johns River, 3, 5, 6, 8, 9, 13, 16, 29, 49, 62
St. Johns and Halifax Railroad, 54
St. Joseph, Fla., 42, 44, 45
St. Lawrence River, 7
St. Marks, 18, 31, 33-37, 39
St. Marks River, 14, 50
St. Marys River, 12, 15, 17
St. Petersburg, Fla., 8, 47, 53, 67, 68, 72, 78
San Augustin (Festival), 6
San Ildefonso, Treaty of, 31, 36
Santa Elena, 6

Santa Rosa Island, 9
Sarasota, Fla., 2
Sardinia, 15
Savannah, Ga., 16, 18, 30
Scotland, 30
Scott, David, 74
Scott, Winfield, 42
Seaboard Coast Line Railroad, 59, 63
Searles, Robert, 12, 17
Sea World, 73
Second Seminole War, 41, 43-45
Seminole, 1
Seminole Indians, 30, 41
Seven Years' War, 17, 18, 21
Shepard, Alan, 73
Sholtz, David, 70, 77
Sicily, 15
Simmons, William H., 39, 45
Sopchoppy, 1
South Carolina, 5, 6, 11, 12, 15, 18, 22, 30, 41,
    44, 47
Space Age, 73
Space Shuttle, 75
Spain, 2-6, 8, 15, 17, 18, 24, 26, 27, 29-31, 33,
    34, 36, 40, 60, 62
Spanish-American War, 61-63
Standard Oil, 60
State College, 54
Steinhatchee, 1
Stinson (airplane), 67
Supreme Court of Florida, 70
Suwannee River, 2, 35

Tallahassee, Fla., 1, 9, 14, 18, 39, 44, 45, 47, 50,
    53, 54, 56
Tamiami Trail, 69, 77
Tampa, Fla., 41, 45, 48, 49, 60, 61, 66, 67, 69,
    71, 77
Tampa Bay, 48, 56
Tampa Bay Hotel, 60
Telogia, 1
Tennessee, 5, 32, 35
Texas, 4, 35, 36
Thompson, Wiley, 41, 45
Thonotosassa, 1
Thopekaliga, 1
Three Friends (ship), 62
Timucua Indians, 2
Tombigbee River, 32
Tonyn, Patrick, 23, 24, 26, 29, 36
Tourism, 72
Trammel, Park, 62
Trapier, James, 49
Tsala Aopoka, 1

Turnbull, Andrew, 23, 24, 26
Tyler, John, 42

Umatilla, 1
United States of America, 5, 7, 11, 24, 29-31, 33,
    36, 37, 39, 41-45, 47, 52, 55, 60, 61, 66, 67,
    70, 71
USS Maine (ship), 60
USS North Carolina (ship), 65
Utina Indians, 2

Valparaiso, 70, 74
Venezuela, 33
Veracruz, 5
Vespucci, Amerigo, 2
Virginia, 11, 18, 35, 51, 53, 68

Wacahoota, 1
Wakulla River, 14, 18
Walls, Josiah, 53, 54, 56
War of 1812, 36
War of the Quadruple Alliance, 15
War of the Spanish Succession, 18
Washington, George, 30, 36
Wausau, 1
Weekiwachee, 1
Welaka, 1
West Florida Seminary, 50
Westcott, James D., Jr., 43
Wetappo, 1
Wewahitchka, 1
White, Edward, 74
Whitehall, 63
Whitted, Albert, 68, 77
Whitted, T. A., Mr. & Mrs., 68
Wild Cat (Coacoochee), 41, 42, 45
Williams, John Lee, 39, 45
Wilson, Woodrow, 65
Wimco, 1
Winchester, Va., 53
Withlacoochee, 1
Works Project Administration (WPA), 70
World War I, 65, 67, 71, 77, 78
World War II, 61, 65, 71, 72, 74
Worth, William Jenkins, 42, 43, 45
Wright, Orville, 67
Wright, Wilbur, 67

Yalaha, 1
Yeehaw, 1
Yorktown, Va., 53
Young, John, 75
Yulee, David Levy, 43, 45
Yulee Sugar Mill, 56